AIR UNIVERSITY

AIR FORCE RESEARCH INSTITUTE

"When You Get a Job to Do, Do It"

The Airpower Leadership of Lt Gen William H. Tunner

DAVID S. HANSON
Lieutenant Colonel, USAF

Drew Paper No. 4

Air University Press
Maxwell Air Force Base, Alabama 36112-5962

May 2008

Muir S. Fairchild Research Information Center Cataloging Data

Hanson, David S., 1969–
    "When you get a job to do, do it" : the airpower leadership of Lt Gen William H. Tunner. / David S. Hanson.
        p. ; cm. – (Drew paper, 1941-3785 ; no. 4)
    Includes bibliographical references.
    ISBN 978-1-58566-183-1.
        1. Tunner, William H.—Military Leadership. 2. United States. Air Force—Officers—Biography. 3. United States. Air Force—Transport service—History. 4. Generals—United States—Biography. 5. Airlift, Military—United States—History. I. Title. II. Series.

    358.40092—dc22

First Printing May 2008
Second Printing April 2011

Disclaimer

This Drew Paper and others in the series are available electronically at the Air University Research Web site http://research.maxwell.af.mil and the AU Press Web site http://aupress.maxwell.af.mil.

The Drew Papers

The Drew Papers are occasional publications sponsored by the Air Force Research Institute (AFRI), Maxwell AFB, Alabama. AFRI publishes this series of papers to commemorate the distinguished career of Col Dennis "Denny" Drew, USAF, retired. In 30 years at Air University, Colonel Drew served on the Air Command and Staff College faculty, directed the Airpower Research Institute, and served as dean, associate dean, and professor of military strategy at the School of Advanced Air and Space Studies, Maxwell AFB. Colonel Drew is one of the Air Force's most extensively published authors and an international speaker in high demand. He has lectured to over 100,000 students at Air University as well as to foreign military audiences. In 1985 he received the Muir S. Fairchild Award for outstanding contributions to Air University. In 2003 Queen Beatrix of the Netherlands made him a Knight in the Order of Orange-Nassau for his contributions to education in the Royal Netherlands Air Force.

The Drew Papers are dedicated to promoting the understanding of air and space power theory and application. These studies are published by the Air University Press and broadly distributed throughout the US Air Force, the Department of Defense, and other governmental organizations, as well as to leading scholars, selected institutions of higher learning, public-policy institutes, and the media.

All military members and civilian employees assigned to Air University are invited to contribute unclassified manuscripts that deal with air and/or space power history, theory, doctrine, or strategy, or with joint or combined service matters bearing on the application of air and/or space power.

Authors should submit three copies of a double-spaced, typed manuscript and an electronic version of the manuscript on removable media along with a brief (200-word maximum) abstract. The electronic file should be compatible with Microsoft Windows and Microsoft Word—Air University Press uses Word as its standard word-processing program.

Please send inquiries or comments to
Director
Air Force Research Institute
155 N. Twining St.
Maxwell AFB, AL 36112-5962
Tel: (334) 953-9587
DSN 493-9587
Fax: (334) 953-6739
DSN 493-6739
E-mail: research.support@maxwell.af.mil

Contents

Illustrations

About the
Author

Lt Col David S. Hanson

Lt Col David S. Hanson graduated from Auburn University with a bachelor's degree in history. He was a Reserve Officer Training Corps distinguished graduate and received a regular commission in 1991. Following undergraduate pilot training at Reese AFB, Texas, he was assigned to the 41st Airlift Squadron at Pope AFB, North Carolina, as a C-130 pilot. Colonel Hanson then moved to Air Force Special Operations Command where he was an evaluator pilot in the AC-130H and the MC-130H. He was later assigned to the 15th Special Operations Squadron and then the 16th Special Operations Squadron at Hurlburt Field, Florida, and also served with the 1st Special Operations Squadron at Kadena AB, Japan. Colonel Hanson is a senior pilot with over 3,200 flying hours. In 2005 he was an outstanding graduate from the USAF Weapons School and took an assignment as an instructor at the 14th Weapons Squadron, Hurlburt Field. In June 2006, he graduated with distinction from the Advanced School of Air Mobility and in 2007 graduated from the School of Advanced Air and Space Studies. Colonel Hanson holds a Master of Aeronautical Science degree from Embry-Riddle Aeronautical University, a Master of Air Mobility degree from the Air Force Institute of Technology and a Master of Airpower Art and Science degree from Air University.

Currently, Colonel Hanson serves as the chief of programming, Headquarters Air Force Special Operations Command at Hurlburt Field. He and his wife, Cindy, have three daughters, Sage, Avery, and Reese.

Acknowledgments

I would like to thank the faculty and staff at the School of Advanced Air and Space Studies (SAASS) for their continued dedication and inspiration in developing future strategists. I would also like to express my appreciation to several key people who contributed to the completion of this study. First, my advisor, Maj Ian Bryan, for his unrelenting advice, support, and dedication. His attention to detail while reviewing my work was extremely valuable and made my writing that much better. Next, I would like to thank Lt Col Phil LaSala for his key inputs and insightful comments. I also want to thank Dr. James Kiras for his guidance and mentorship throughout the completion of this project and my SAASS academic year.

In addition, I want to acknowledge Toni Russ at the Air Force Historical Research Agency at Maxwell AFB, Alabama, and Bob Christensen at the Air Force Doctrine Center at Maxwell Air Force Base, for taking time to provide me with important information, inputs, and insight.

Most importantly, I would like to thank my wife, Cindy, and daughters, Sage, Avery, and Reese, for their patience and understanding as I completed this project. Without their love and support this study would not have been possible.

DAVID S. HANSON, Lt Col, USAF
Chief, Programming Branch
Headquarters Air Force Special
Operations Command

Chapter 1

Introduction

The actual operation of a successful airlift is about as glamorous as drops of water on stone. There's no frenzy, no flap, just the inexorable process of getting the job done.

—Lt Gen William H. Tunner

Throughout the brief history of military aviation and the United States Air Force, there have been many great leaders. Several, such as Mitchell, Foulois, Spaatz, and Arnold, built the foundation for military aviation and championed an independent air force. Others, such as LeMay, Quesada, and Schriever, shaped the Air Force and developed specific elements of air and space power.[1] While these leaders tend to be revered and studied by military professionals attending Air Force advanced education programs, Lt Gen William H. Tunner and his contributions to the airlift element of airpower do not receive similar attention and are typically underappreciated. Thus, a question arises: Was Tunner a successful Air Force leader? This question is answered using a framework that builds upon current Air Force leadership doctrine to examine and critique Tunner's military career during the interwar years, World War II, and early Cold War.

Gen Curtis LeMay described Tunner as "the transportation expert to end transportation experts."[2] As a graduate of the US Military Academy in 1928, Tunner pursued a career in aviation and gained valuable experience as an Army Air Corps pilot, leader, and staff officer during the interwar period. In 1941, this experience landed him a job on the staff of the newly formed Ferrying Command, which held the critical responsibility of moving aircraft from US factories to American and Allied combat units overseas. A year later, when Ferrying Command was expanded and reorganized into Air Transport Command (ATC), Tunner was chosen to command Ferrying Division. These early experiences and leadership opportunities provided Tunner with a strong foundation in air mobility.

From 1944 to 1949, Tunner leveraged his expertise in air transportation to successfully command the "Hump" airlift operation and the Berlin airlift. Tunner thereafter served in a variety of Air Force leadership positions that included command of Combat Cargo Command during the Korean War, command of US Air Forces in Europe, and command of the Military Air Transport Service (MATS). As the MATS commander, he pressed for the development of a modern mobility aircraft fleet, resulting in the modernization of existing aircraft and the development and procurement of the C-141. While these later stages of Tunner's career are worthy of study, this paper focuses on his experience and actions up to 1949 and his performance as a leader while commanding two historic airlift campaigns.

Air Force Leadership Doctrine

Air Force doctrine represents the beliefs held by the service about how best to accomplish a task. According to Air Force Doctrine Document (AFDD) 1-1, *Leadership and Force Development*, doctrine is "distilled through experience and passed from one generation of Airmen to the next."[3] General LeMay goes further by stating, "At the very heart of warfare lies doctrine. It represents the central beliefs for waging war in order to achieve victory. Doctrine is of the mind, a network of faith and knowledge reinforced by experience which lays the pattern for the utilization of men, equipment, and tactics. It is the building material for strategy. It is fundamental to sound judgment."[4]

The origins of Air Force leadership doctrine can be traced to the publication of Air Force Manual 35-15, *Leadership*, in 1948. This manual intended to establish a leadership doctrine distinct from the Army's that outlined the "missions, roles, functions, and guiding principles of the Air Force and incorporate[d] details of the latest scientific findings on leadership."[5] AFDD 1-1 represents the most current evolution of Air Force leadership doctrine and is designed to assist Airmen in "fulfilling their assigned duties and leadership responsibilities."[6]

AFDD 1-1 defines leadership as the "art and science of influencing and directing people to accomplish the assigned mission."[7] While mission accomplishment is often considered the primary task of a military organization, it is important to understand that it is the organization's people that perform the mission. AFDD 1-1 states, "Effective leadership transforms human potential into effective performance in the present and prepares capable leaders for the future."[8] Thus, current Air Force leadership guidance identifies a leader's dual responsibilities as successfully accomplishing the mission while at the same time developing people.

While AFDD 1-1 identifies personal experience, leadership competencies, and leadership actions as the components associated with effective Air Force leadership, it does not clearly define these leadership components or present a useful relationship between them. For example, AFDD 1-1 falls short in clearly describing leadership competencies. Instead, "leadership" is merely coupled with the words: abilities, acumen, beliefs, bench-strength, capabilities, competencies, performance, philosophy, principles, qualities, responsibilities, roles, skills, style, tasks, techniques, and traits. These terms seem to be used interchangeably. Additionally, the correlation between the various leadership components is confusing and is not depicted in a useful structural arrangement. While this study's intention is not to critique AFDD 1-1, it does address some of its weaknesses and highlights Air Force leadership doctrine as an area ripe for development.

Proposed Air Force Leadership Framework

Using AFDD 1-1 as a foundational reference, this study proposes an Air Force leadership framework, presented in figure 1. This framework simplifies the concepts presented in AFDD 1-1 and highlights the relationships between Air Force leadership components and the results they produce.

The proposed Air Force leadership framework used in this study organizes the three main components found in AFDD 1-1: experience, leadership competencies, and leadership actions. Experience forms the foundation for Air Force leadership and is established during initial military education and training and developed through operational practice. For most Airmen, building experience is the principal focus during their early career. Early education, training, and operational experience help Airmen work together within the Air Force and develop skills in their assigned specialty. A breadth of experience broadens Airmen's understanding of the Air Force and equips them to apply

Figure 1. Air Force Leadership Framework (Proposed) (Adapted from Air Force Doctrine Document [AFDD] 1-1, *Leadership and Force Development*, 18 February 2006.)

unique personal knowledge to different situations. Depth of experience aids in developing professional expertise. According to AFDD 1-1, competence and credibility require a depth of experience as a foundation for effective leadership.[9]

As military leaders progress to positions of increased responsibility, they build upon their leadership foundations through the development of leadership competencies. Leadership competencies represent the skills, knowledge, qualifications, and capacity that are required for the leadership level involved. AFDD 1-1 identifies three leadership levels within the Air Force: tactical, operational, and strategic, and states that each level "requires a different mix of competencies and experience."[10] In describing the relationship between levels and competencies, AFDD 1-1 states that "while all aspects of the competencies are necessary to varying degrees at all levels, there is a change in focus based on the level at which a leader is operating."[11] As such, tactical leaders use personal competencies that focus on face-to-face interpersonal relations. Operational leaders center on people/team competencies that facilitate team relationships. Leaders at the strategic level focus on institutional competencies that establish influence, structure, and vision, both internal and external, to the organization.[12] In describing the progressive development of leadership competencies, AFDD 1-1 states that the competencies "needed at successively higher echelons in the Air Force build on those learned at previous levels."[13]

Finally, experience and leadership competencies provide the basis for the leadership actions of Airmen. According to AFDD 1-1, leadership actions provide a means for Air Force leaders to "influence people, improve their abilities, and direct their activities to accomplish their military mission."[14] Leaders influence through their capability to communicate effectively, motivate people, set standards, and act decisively. Leaders improve their organization by institutionalizing successful practices, providing challenging experiences, and fostering their subordinates' growth. According to AFDD 1-1, leaders are responsible for mentoring and developing more leaders.[15] Thus, leadership actions directly influence the results associated with the responsibilities of an Air Force leader.

According to the Air Force leadership doctrine, the leadership components associated with the Air Force leadership framework developed for this study provide the means for Airmen to achieve excellence. Given a strong foundation of professional and technical experience, enduring leadership competencies, and effective leadership actions, Air Force leaders can produce immediate and lasting results. While this framework provides guidance for the development of future Air Force leaders, it is also a tool for analyzing the past. This study employs the framework to evaluate the success of General Tunner's leadership.

Research Overview

Using the components identified in AFDD 1-1 and the structure proposed in the Air Force leadership framework, the succeeding chapters examine General Tunner as an Air Force leader. Chapter 2 describes key elements of Tunner's early experiences that provided the foundation for his leadership development. Chapter 3 explores the maturing of Tunner's leadership competencies, beginning with his assignment to the newly established Air Corps Ferrying Command and following his rapid progression from personnel officer to commanding general of Ferrying Division. This study examines Tunner's leadership actions during the Hump airlift in chapter 4, and the Berlin airlift in chapter 5. Chapter 6 provides a summary and a critique of Tunner's life and leadership.

Notes

(All notes appear in shortened form. For full details, see the appropriate entry in the bibliography.)

1. The Air Force leaders mentioned include: Maj Gen William "Billy" Mitchell, Maj Gen Benjamin D. Foulois, Gen Carl T. Spaatz, Gen Henry H. "Hap" Arnold, Gen Curtis E. LeMay, Lt Gen Elwood R. Quesada, and Gen Bernard A. Schriever.
2. LeMay, *Mission with LeMay*, 416.
3. Air Force Doctrine Document (AFDD) 1, *Air Force Basic Doctrine*, 17 November 2003, 1.
4. Ibid.
5. Brown, "The Sources of Leadership Doctrine."
6. AFDD 1-1, *Leadership and Force Development*, iii.
7. Ibid., 1.
8. Ibid.
9. Ibid., 25–26.
10. Ibid., 8.
11. Ibid.
12. Ibid., 9.
13. Ibid., 8–10.
14. Ibid., 11.
15. Ibid.

Chapter 2

Education, Training, and Experience

I'm firmly convinced that leaders are not born; they're educated, trained, and made, as in every other profession. To ensure a strong, ready Air Force, we must always remain dedicated to this process.

—Gen Curtis E. LeMay

William Henry Tunner was born 14 July 1906 in Elizabeth, New Jersey. As one of five children, he grew up in a household of limited means. His parents stressed education and by the time he was in high school, they had already sent three of his siblings to college. As William's turn approached, he realized the expense would strain the family's finances. He stumbled upon a solution during a high school civics class: an appointment to the United States Military Academy at West Point, New York. He wrote to his congressman, studied hard, and attended additional classes to prepare for the exam.[1] Unlike some congressmen who used less discriminating means of selecting their appointees to West Point, Congressman Ernest R. Ackerman used a competitive process. As Tunner said, "He used the Civil Service examination to determine the grade, and he gave the appointment to the man who had the best one. That happened to be me."[2]

Tunner was selected for an appointment to West Point on 26 January 1924 and reported for admission on 1 July. During an October 1976 interview, Lieutenant General Tunner was asked to comment on hazing during his first year at West Point. He stated, "There is a place for it. . . . In the military a man has got to respond immediately to the wishes of his superiors without question, just as he's ordered. . . . We responded immediately; delay meant punishment, and so we got into the habit of doing exactly what we were told to the best of our ability when we were told."[3]

Tunner's initial interest in flying and first exposure to the Air Corps occurred during his senior year at the academy. During

7

an orientation week at Mitchell Field, New York, he was able to fly in five different airplane types and remembers "each flight as a thrilling experience."[4] Tunner knew what he wanted, and on 9 June 1928 he was commissioned as a second lieutenant in the Army, assigned to the Air Corps.[5]

Lieutenant Tunner attended Air Corps flight school at Brooks and Kelly Fields in Texas from September 1928 to September 1929.[6] He described flight training as "a terrific thrill to get up in an airplane, all by yourself, and realize that you could fly. It was a feeling of mastery."[7] While Tunner may have felt mastery, his flight school training reports and early flying experience did not reflect it. His ground school performance was average, and his flying grades were consistently "satisfactory," the lowest passing mark.[8] When asked about his final check flight, which was flown with Claire Chennault, Tunner simply stated, "He passed me."[9]

Upon completion of flight training, Lieutenant Tunner was assigned to the 11th Bomb Squadron at Rockwell Field, California, where he first became involved in air transport. About a month out of flight school, the operations officer called Tunner in and told him to fly a three-engine Fokker from Rockwell Field to a maintenance depot in Sacramento, California. While he had never flown this type of aircraft, Tunner was eager to fly almost anything in order to gain experience and log flying hours. His preflight checks began with a walk-around inspection of the aircraft. He entered the airplane to continue his checks and was surprised to find the cabin full of passengers. "The eager, shining face of a twenty-three-year-old second lieutenant could hardly have inspired my passengers with confidence," Tunner later recalled.[10] There were no experienced pilots around to explain the Fokker, so Tunner received his cockpit introduction from an aircraft mechanic kind enough to point out the various aircraft controls, instruments, and gauges. Equally as brief was his preflight planning, since there was no requirement for a flight plan, no weather information, and the only map available was a California state map.[11] This left a mark on Tunner: "Though I thought nothing of my first transport flight then, I have certainly recalled it many times over the years since . . . to make sure that no other pilot or crew member . . . under my command would be checked out with such casualness."[12]

While successful in his first air-transport mission and rated an excellent airplane pilot on his initial efficiency report, his rating fell to satisfactory within a few months. In contrast, Tunner's performance as squadron supply officer rose from satisfactory to excellent.[13] These trends in flying and staff performance would continue.

Lieutenant Tunner was next assigned to Randolph Field, Texas, as a flying instructor, a duty for which he was not well suited. Within a few months he was relieved from instructor duties for temperamental incapacity and an alleged fear of flying, having stated that he found his whole class of students incapable of handling an aircraft.[14] While his initial efficiency report rated him as a satisfactory flying instructor, the details stated that he was "not particularly adaptable as a flying instructor but well equipped for . . . other duties."[15] Tunner's other efficiency reports from Randolph only rate him as a satisfactory airplane pilot, indicating that he did not return to his duties as a flight instructor. While at Randolph, Tunner broadened his experience with additional duties that included squadron supply officer, adjutant, engineering and operations officer, and mess officer.[16]

In January of 1935, First Lieutenant Tunner reported for duty to the 7th Observation Squadron at France Field in the Panama Canal Zone. The Air Corps mission in Panama was to defend the Canal Zone from a perceived German threat in South America and from an attack on the Panama Canal by the Japanese navy.[17] This formidable mission required building, organizing, maintaining, and supplying airpower in the Canal Zone.[18] While his initial duties included squadron adjutant, supply officer, and airplane pilot, Tunner's previous staff experience, expertise, and interests vaulted him into broader, more challenging tasks. Within a year of arriving, Tunner advanced to the 19th Composite Wing as assistant wing operations officer and officer in charge of the air warning service and airdrome maintenance.[19] By December of 1936, he was serving as the base's operations officer and intelligence officer.[20] As an operations officer, Tunner enjoyed coordinating the scheduling and maintenance of aircraft and the scheduling and training of personnel.

His duties as an intelligence officer centered on the support of the Antiaircraft Intelligence Service (AAIS) associated with

9

the Canal Zone. Radar had not yet been developed, so the AAIS warned of approaching enemy aircraft. AAIS troops were stationed at isolated jungle outposts approximately ten miles apart along both coasts of Panama. If spotters saw unknown or unfriendly aircraft, the information would be radioed to the commander of the Canal Zone. Tunner ran the school that trained the AAIS radio operators to send coded messages, and he organized the building of outlying airfields to resupply the AAIS outposts.[21] His final efficiency report from France Field rated Lieutenant Tunner as superior in all areas, described him as an exceedingly capable officer, and recommended him for training at the Air Corps' premiere training program, the Air Corps Tactical School (ACTS).[22]

In February 1937, Lieutenant Tunner was reassigned to the 16th Observation Squadron at Lawson Field, Fort Benning, Georgia, and served as a pilot and as the unit's operations officer. The squadron operated the air field and conducted a variety of missions to support the Infantry School at Fort Benning.[23] There were five aircraft and eight pilots tasked with familiarizing Infantry School students with Air Corps airplanes and tactics.[24] While assigned to Lawson Field, the newly promoted Captain Tunner learned about ground forces tactics. Again, he earned the highest marks on his efficiency reports, which highlighted his ability to "inspire confidence and to exert an inspiring influence on the younger officers serving with him."[25] Following his assignment at Lawson Field, Captain Tunner attended the ACTS, where he earned an excellent rating, and then proceeded to his first command.[26]

Command of the Memphis Air Corps Detachment provided unique opportunities and experiences for Captain Tunner. His primary duty was to locate young civilian airline pilots, weekend fliers, and crop dusters, and encourage them to become reserve officers in the Air Corps.[27] This entailed identifying candidates, providing them with courses on military aviation, and helping them get commissioned.[28] Additionally, his detachment was responsible for military operations at Memphis Municipal Airport, Tennessee, which confronted him with problems that usually faced commanders of larger Air Corps bases. One of his responsibilities was to ensure the servicing of transient military aircraft. Tunner stated that "with a good crew of mechanics well provided for, and a supply section that functioned well under firm supervision, I was able to get these duties carried out with a performance record which was routinely high."[29] It was on one such stopover at Tunner's base that the Air Corps chief of the personnel division met with Captain Tunner and toured Tunner's detachment. "When he came back from the West Coast where he was going, he stopped over again and said, 'By the way, I'm having you reassigned to Washington to my office.'"[30] This was not the assignment Tunner had in mind.

On 16 February 1941, Tunner reported to the Air Corps Personnel Division and pinned on the rank of major. He also managed an attached status at nearby Bolling Field, Washington, DC, in order to continue flying.[31] "The important job for which I left Memphis turned out to be sitting in an office writing orders moving airplanes around. I had nothing to do with who went where; I merely took the memorandum concerning the airplane, found a driver among the sixteen-hundred pilots then in the Air Corps, then wrote an official order telling him to fly it from where it was to where it was supposed to go."[32]

At times when there were no pilots available, Major Tunner would write orders for himself to fly the mission. He normally flew on weekends to avoid missing time in the office. Typically, these missions involved a cross-country flight delivering an aircraft from a manufacturing facility on the west coast to a modifications center or Air Corps flying unit.[33] "I made these trips entirely for fun, with no idea that I'd someday be in the ferrying business, where this experience would prove helpful."[34] After just four months in Washington, Major Tunner was reassigned to the newly established Air Corps Ferrying Command, where his education, training, and experience would prove invaluable.

Notes

1. Tunner, *Over the Hump*, 6.
2. Tunner, oral history interview, 1–2.
3. Ibid., 3.
4. Tunner, *Over the Hump*, 6.
5. Form No. 0337.A, Adjutant General's Office (AGO), "Historical Record of Officer."
6. "Major General William Henry Tunner, USAF, 374A (Record of Service as of 3 July 1953)."

7. Tunner, *Over the Hump*, 7.

8. Air Corps Primary Flying School, "Final Grade Sheet."

9. Tunner, oral history interview, 7.

10. Tunner, *Over the Hump*, 4.

11. Ibid.

12. Ibid., 8.

13. War Department (WD), AGO Form No. 67, 1 July 1930–30 June 1931.

14. Gorgas Hospital, "Abstract of Clinical Records."

15. WD, AGO Form No. 67, 23 October 1931–27 February 1932.

16. Ibid., 1 July 1933–30 June 1934; and "Major General William Henry Tunner, USAF, 374A (Record of Service as of 3 July 1953)."

17. Tunner, oral history interview, 9–11; and Coira, oral history interview, 9.

18. VI Bomber Command History, 6.

19. WD, AGO Form No. 67, 26 September 1935–30 June 1936.

20. Ibid., 31 December 1936–21 April 1937.

21. Tunner, oral history interview, 9–11.

22. WD, AGO Form No. 67, 31 December 1936–21 April 1937.

23. Flight "B," 16th Observation Squadron, "To: 1st Lt William H. Tunner."

24. Tunner, oral history interview, 13.

25. WD, AGO Form No. 67, 1 July 1938–30 June 1939.

26. Ibid., 7 September 1939–5 December 1939.

27. Tunner, *Over the Hump*, 13.

28. Tunner, oral history interview, 14.

29. Tunner, *Over the Hump*, 14.

30. Tunner, oral history interview, 15–16.

31. Office of the Chief of the Air Corps, "Personnel Orders," 17 February 1941.

32. Tunner, *Over the Hump*, 17.

33. Office of the Chief of the Air Corps, "To: Maj William H. Tunner, 31 May 1941."

34. Tunner, *Over the Hump*, 18.

Chapter 3

Leadership Competencies

If you get a job to do, do it.

—Lt Gen William H. Tunner

America's attitude toward the war in Europe changed dramatically in 1940, and by the end of the year Pres. Franklin D. Roosevelt favored "all aid short of war" for Britain.[1] By the middle of March 1941, Britain made up for its lack of preparation in both manufacturing and materials as a result of the cash-and-carry and Lend-Lease programs.[2] The Royal Air Force (RAF) Ferry Command picked up American-built aircraft at transfer points in Canada from American crews. On 28 May 1941, President Roosevelt assigned responsibility for delivering Lend-Lease aircraft to the secretary of war and stated that he was certain that the United States could get bombers to England quickly.[3] The following day, the Army Air Corps began organizing the Ferrying Command and assigned Col Robert Olds as commander.[4]

Colonel Olds was ideal for the job. He was described as "a man of fire, drive, and courage," with an "unusual grasp of the national and international background of his new mission. He was intolerant of failure or obstructionism, won the loyalty of his subordinates and was unafraid of his superiors."[5] Olds believed in delegating authority and trusting subordinates, both of which became characteristics of the new command and its young staff, where Major Tunner served as personnel officer.

Tunner did not give much credit to Robert Olds for influencing him, though they shared many similar characteristics. General LeMay described Olds as having the greatest impact on his 35-year career. Having worked for Olds as a young officer, LeMay stated, "I began to get an insight under him as to what leadership meant and the great amount of work that had to be done to build a first class Air Force."[6] While there is some indication that the Ferrying Command was intended to be temporary, it is likely that Colonel Olds' strong personality and his clear vision of his organization's purpose were the driving factors in its rapid growth and its permanent establishment.

One of Major Tunner's initial challenges as the Ferrying Command's personnel officer was to ensure that there were sufficient pilots and crew members available to the organization to maintain a steadily increasing flow of aircraft. During its first few weeks, the Ferrying Command needed to use civilian factory pilots.[7] Within a month, however, Tunner shifted primarily to Air Corps crews to maximize their flying experience and training and to better utilize available Air Corps personnel. Though National Guard and reserve crew members were initially used, it became necessary to assign pilots from throughout the Air Corps to temporary duty with the Ferrying Command.[8] According to Tunner, "everything pertaining to those pilots and the pilots we already had and the training of new pilots was passing through my hands."[9]

To help crews conduct safe and effective operations, the Ferrying Command established its own regulations and operating instructions. Regulations established minimum weather standards, maximum operating altitudes, and position reporting procedures for ferrying crews.[10] The Ferrying Command's first operating instruction identified minimum crew requirements and required flying qualifications for different aircraft categories ranging from heavy bombardment to smaller Cessna aircraft.[11] These regulations and instructions guided every aspect of getting the aircraft to the transfer points in Canada for the handoff to Allied pilots.

Rapid production was not the only factor to contend with. Further complicating the Ferrying Command's mission was the way aircraft were assembled. Tunner noticed that "each airplane was often ferried three and four times. The reason was, all airplanes were pushed out of the factory as soon as they could fly, and they all needed modifications—radios, guns, armament, perhaps sometime changes in the landing gear—all sorts of modifications. These modifications took place in various cities of the United States."[12] A detailed route structure allowed for transporting aircraft between factories and transfer points (figure 2). Control points tracked aircraft movements and provided minor maintenance and enroute support.[13] At the installation points, aircraft inspections and equipment

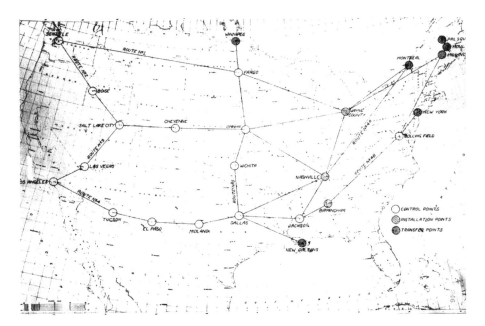

Figure 2. Ferrying Command Control, Installation, and Transfer Points.
(Reprinted from Air Transport Command, *The Origins of the Ferrying Division,*
vol. 1, *The Air Corps Ferrying Command, May through December 1941.*
301.01 V.1, 29 May 1941–30 September 1945, 00180381, Air Force Historical
Research Agency [AFHRA], Maxwell AFB, AL, 246.)

installations ensured transfer of complete airplanes. Finally,
an aircraft arriving at its transfer point underwent a final inspection before being delivered to the British Ferry Command
for flight to its final destination.[14]

After delivering an aircraft to a transfer point, the ferrying crew
and its equipment normally returned to base via commercial
aircraft.[15] Initially, this was the factory from which the crew had
last departed, where they would wait for their next assignment.
"It frequently happened that at one factory pilots would be sitting around waiting for planes to come off the production line
while at the same time planes would be ready and waiting at
another factory with no pilots to fly them."[16] Tunner saw the
need for an organization on the west coast that would be responsible for putting pilots where they were needed. Borrowing a
page out of Colonel Olds' playbook, Tunner took the initiative to
acquire Long Beach Reserve Base, California, for the Ferrying

Command.[17] Although Olds was furious when he found out that he had a base to run, this acquisition proved to be valuable.

In addition to his duties as personnel officer, Major Tunner became the executive officer for the Ferrying Command. He assisted in setting up the command's headquarters, and by the end of November 1941, Ferrying Command crews were flying a steady stream of aircraft to Canada. This changed on 7 December 1941, as the Japanese attack on Pearl Harbor brought America fully into the war, which required significant transformations within the Ferrying Command. Tunner recalled that "after Pearl Harbor all ferrying stopped with a bang. Every pilot we had borrowed from any other unit, except the National Guard and Reserve, was ordered to return to his command, and to return immediately."[18] He continued, "It was obvious that the plane-ferrying business was in for a great expansion. We had to have pilots, but it was now obvious that we were not going to get them from the military. Fortunately, from my experience in Memphis I knew that there were many pilots, good pilots, out there in the civilian world. I had the idea that they would rather deliver planes for us than be drafted into the infantry. I put out word that we intended to hire as many civilian pilots as we could get."[19] The hiring began in December, and by the end of January 1942, between 350 and 400 civilian pilots were ferrying aircraft.[20] This new source of manpower required changes to the organization.

Just as Colonel Olds had established the culture and guidance, Tunner developed the way forward. "We simply had to decentralize, I realized we had to have some form of organization by which routine decisions could be made at a lower level instead of piling up in Washington. I took pencil and paper and, in an hour or so, tore the command apart and put it back together again in a simple little chart, setting up a general headquarters, a Domestic Division, and a Foreign Division."[21] Colonel Olds approved Major Tunner's concept for reorganizing the Ferrying Command and placed the command's operations officer, Maj Tom Mosley, in charge of the Foreign Division. On 28 December 1941, Tunner took command of the Domestic Division and was promoted to lieutenant colonel.[22]

With this reorganization, Foreign Division developed overseas flight routes, carried cargo and passengers, and monitored troop and aircraft movements over Ferrying Command

16

routes, while Domestic Division managed all domestic flying, to include Lend-Lease aircraft and those destined for the Air Corps units.[23] The initial planned personnel strength of the Domestic Division included 134 officers, 2,720 enlisted personnel, and approximately 600 crews.[24]

Lieutenant Colonel Tunner encouraged his young staff to take initiative and responsibility. "If you get a job to do, do it," he told them.[25] Additionally, he stressed that his staff should coordinate as a team and bring only difficult problems to him. He insisted on being informed of all important developments in his command. Weekly meetings encouraged staff communication, and inspection trips kept Tunner connected with those in the field. It was his belief that "if things were not perfect out in the field, it reflected on the headquarters of the Domestic Wing, since the latter was the supervising body."[26]

The Domestic Division faced a lack of qualified aircrew, maintenance, and administrative personnel. This resulted in the widespread hiring of civilian pilots in early 1942.[27] Tunner and his staff had to organize, train, and equip the new fliers and contend with the dramatic increase in aircraft production, both in number and type.

Tunner drew on his recruiting experience in Memphis to identify good civilian pilots and get them commissioned. Within a month of taking command, he outlined the basic requirements, to include age, education, physical ability, and flying experience needed for Ferrying Command service.[28] A week later Tunner had established procedures and criteria for commissioning civilian fliers as service pilots in the Ferrying Command. After meeting the basic service requirements, civilian pilots faced a board of military pilots who conducted interviews and made recommendations as to the rank the new pilots would receive.[29] For example, a civilian between the ages of 21 and 35 who met the basic requirement of 300 hours flight time was commissioned as a second lieutenant, while a man between 28 and 42 with 2,000 hours of multi-engine time became a captain.[30] These pilots received the aeronautical rating and wings of a "service pilot," which was specifically for the civilians in the Ferrying Command since they were not Air Corps flight school graduates.[31] Though most had flown single-engine planes, the service pilots transitioned to military aircraft without difficulty.

While civilians provided necessary manpower, they also presented early difficulties. The first ferrying mission by these pilots took nine P-40s from the aircraft factory in Buffalo, New York, to San Antonio, Texas. There was no one available to train the service pilots on the P-40 at the factory, so their aircraft qualification officially occurred at an en route stop where an Air Corps officer stated, "You must be able to fly the P-40s—you got them here." One of the nine, however, failed to complete the mission.

Civilian pilots were unfamiliar with military procedures and Air Corps flying regulations. According to the Air Transport Command history, "There were irregularities in complying with regulations about clearances, forms pertinent to military traffic, responsibilities of flight leaders and pilots, safeguarding the aircraft while in transit, what airdromes were to be used, and other regulations in which military pilots were thoroughly schooled."[32] These early challenges required that, along with the ferrying mission, the Domestic Division take on additional training of Ferrying Command pilots.

Lieutenant Colonel Tunner began by reorganizing the division. Working with the Air Staff in Washington, he was able to shift pilots from dispersed aircraft factories to centrally located bases within various sectors. He explained that the "progressive training of pilots requires that they be continuously checked off on new and different types of aircraft," and that this "would be impossible if pilots were stationed at factories."[33]

Next, Tunner established transition schools at each sector. These schools were responsible for the transition training associated with aircraft qualifications and aircrew ground training. A basic system for classifying pilots, which included "four-engine," "two-engine," "pursuit," and "other," was established, and it was mandatory that pilots acquire necessary flight time to meet the requirements to check out into higher classifications.[34] To support flight training, Tunner worked with the director of War Organization and Movement and placed training aircraft at each sector. This dramatically increased the training hours flown from 1,083 training hours in January to 6,482 in June.[35]

In conjunction with aircrew flight training, ground school was also an important part of the transition training program. In this area, Tunner ruled that "if a pilot was at his home base only one day he need not attend classes, but if he was there for two or more days he should have one day off and spend the others in school."[36] By organizing into sectors, establishing transition schools, and acquiring training aircraft, Tunner provided the means to overcome early difficulties and improve his crews' capabilities.

While the quantity and quality of Domestic Division aircrews were improving, Tunner still faced ever-increasing ferrying requirements. A major problem was getting pilots home after a ferrying mission in time to perform their next mission.[37] While commercial air and rail transportation were initially used, they were not always available at ferrying destinations and within a few months had become overtaxed by Domestic Division requests. Tunner's solution involved establishing a Crew Transport Service within the Domestic Division. He coordinated with Colonel Olds to set aside some transport aircraft and developed a system of regular service. Within a few months, Tunner was running his own military airline.[38]

The spring of 1942 brought a variety of changes and challenges for Tunner and the Ferrying Command: Tunner was promoted to colonel; he received a new boss, Col Harold George who replaced Colonel Olds; and the command began another reorganization. General Orders No. 8 directed that the Ferrying Command be redesignated as the Air Transport Command, which would consist of two major divisions: the Ferrying Division, and Air Transport Division.[39] Colonel Tunner took command of the newly established Ferrying Division, which was to conduct both the domestic and foreign ferrying missions.[40] Personality conflicts between Colonel Tunner and Col Tom Mosley, the commander of the former Foreign Division, may have contributed to the formation of one division responsible for all ferrying. Mosley was "likable, hearty, and outspoken," though he did not possess Tunner's organizational skills. In contrast, Tunner was "cold and distant but astute and intelligent." The friction between the two grew as complaints surfaced about the condition of the aircraft Tunner's domestic wing delivered to Mosley's foreign wing. Colonel Mosley could not have been happy at the elimination of his wing and the reassignment of the foreign mission to Colonel Tunner.[41]

While Tunner's wing established a strong foundation for domestic ferrying operations, the continuous increase in the types and numbers of aircraft being produced provided a variety of challenges for the new Ferrying Division. Unlike most pilots who fly one type of aircraft, Tunner's task was to have "a pilot for every plane that was made, over every route that was flown, to every fighting front."[42] Reflecting on this undertaking, he stated that "during the course of the war our pilots were called upon to fly a total of some hundred and fifty different models."[43] To match pilot qualifications and aircraft types, Colonel Tunner continued to emphasize training. Building on his early efforts, he developed six classifications for Ferrying Division pilots (table 1), established stringent upgrade qualification requirements, and continued to expand the transition schools. For example, the 2nd Ferrying Group went from only three dedicated training aircraft to 30 by the end of 1943.[44] In addition to the transition schools, the division operated four specialized units that focused on training crews to fly transport, pursuit, and bomber aircraft.[45] A strong indication of the success of the training program came in February 1943 when the organization took over the training mission for the entire Air Transport Command.[46]

Table 1. Ferrying Division pilot qualification classes and requirements

Pilot Classification	Qualification To Fly:
Class I	Low-powered single-engine planes
Class II	Twin-engine trainers and utility planes
Class III	Twin-engine cargo and medium transports, and on instruments
Class IV	Twin-engine planes in advanced categories, such as medium bombers and heavy transports
Class V	The biggest planes, four-engine bombers and transports with overseas delivery
Class P	Single engine, high-performance pursuits or fighters

Adapted from W. H. Tunner, *Over the Hump* (Washington, DC: Office of Air Force History, 1964), 27–28.

Among the initiatives pioneered by the division, Colonel Tunner viewed the flying safety program to be one of his most important contributions. In his view, "The success of the ferrying mission depended upon the number of airplanes safely delivered to their destinations. Every damaged or 'washed-out' plane contributed to the objectives of the enemy just as definitely as though it were destroyed in combat."[47] He emphasized mission and safety as he described the mind-set desired in his pilots: "Our pilots were not supposed to risk their lives or their ships, but to fly skillfully and safely deliver those planes in good condition. The ferry pilot was not expected to be a hero, but just to do his job."[48]

Based on the way major insurance companies were conducting industrial inspections, Tunner believed the Air Corps could benefit from a similar kind of program to support flying safety. He explained that this program would "prevent accidents by continually reviewing the procedures of other departments, but when an accident did occur, flying safety committees were formed to determine and review the causes and to recommend future action to be taken to prevent repetition."[49] This included communicating lessons learned through "accident of the week" postings on squadron bulletin boards and making recommendations for grounding an aircraft type due to poor design and construction.[50] The flying safety program aided in safely delivering "thousands of planes across all of the oceans in every type and kind of weather with an astoundingly low accident rate."[51]

As the Ferrying Division worked to meet the growing number of domestic and foreign ferrying requirements, Colonel Tunner struggled to get enough qualified pilots for his expanding organization. Civilian pilots continued to provide the main source of manpower for the division. During 1942, the division hired 1,730 civilian pilots, of which 1,372 were commissioned into the Air Corps.[52] The British RAF Ferry Command and the Royal Canadian Air Force loaned some crews in 1942 and 1943.[53]

Perhaps the most original approach to manpower taken by Tunner involved redefining the term itself. On 6 September 1942, the Ferrying Division sent a telegram to 83 women who held commercial pilot licenses, explaining the division's desire to use women pilots for domestic ferrying. By the end of October, the Women's Auxiliary Ferrying Squadron (WAFS) had been established, and women were flying airplanes for the division.[54] The Women Airforce Service Pilots (WASP), as they were later named, flew many types of aircraft, including pursuit, bomber, and transport. In late 1944, they delivered almost all of the 2nd Ferrying Group's pursuit aircraft, including P-38s, P-46s, and

P-51s.[55] When he was asked, "How did their record stack up against the men? Were they about equal?" Tunner stated, "No, they were better. Their accident rate was better; their delivery rate was better . . . Women, I found, would do what they were told to do. The young men we had hired with little military training often found excuses and generally, I might say, they were not as good. They were not as well trained. They were not as knowledgeable as the women pilots."[56]

As the Ferrying Division assumed the foreign ferrying mission, it was well prepared. In April 1942, a training program called "Project 32" began to prepare domestic wing pilots for transoceanic flights. This program included transition training, night navigation flights to Cuba, and temporary duty assigned to the foreign wing. "Many problems had to be surmounted by this pioneering group, including airplane breakdowns, lack of repair facilities and personnel, poor weather facilities, improper briefing, and the difficult problem of navigating over the Pacific with its sparse islands and landing fields."[57] Whether Tunner had intended to gain control of all ferrying operations from the beginning is unclear, but when the division took over the foreign mission, these crews provided experience in overseas ferrying and formed the nucleus of the first three foreign ferrying squadrons.[58]

The rapid growth would continue for the next few years, as would the pace of Tunner's career. During its first year, the organization delivered 3,609 aircraft to foreign destinations and completed 54,947 domestic movements.[59] By April 1943, the division consisted of over 20,800 personnel and operated nine main bases in the United States.[60] Tunner had established a means of consistently securing qualified aircrew members, had demonstrated the benefits associated with a dedicated flight safety program, and had been given responsibility for training all pilots within the Air Transport Command. On 30 June 1943, a mere 18 months after donning the rank of major, Tunner was promoted to brigadier general.

The growth, expansion, and increasing responsibilities through the summer of 1943 would continue into 1944. Aircraft delivery requirements continued to rise as the division delivered 12,500 aircraft overseas and 110,000 domestically over the next year.[61] Procurement and training of aircrew and personnel also expanded, and by July 1944, the Ferrying Division numbered more than 45,000 individuals.[62] During the second year of his command, General Tunner continued to introduce innovations that increased his division's contributions to the war effort.

In November 1943, General Tunner created a foreign transport service designed to quickly move vital cargo, supplies, mail, and passengers in support of Allied operations in Europe and Asia. This service consisted of three regularly scheduled runs—the Fireball to India via the South Atlantic, the Crescent to India via the Azores, and the Snowball to the United Kingdom over the North Atlantic.[63] In an effort to expedite aircraft movement on the Crescent run, Tunner set up what he called a "pony-express type operation," where fresh crews took over at points along the route. He explained that "the plane itself went straight through, from America to its final destination, without the delaying transfer of passengers or cargo."[64]

In April 1944, as a complement to the Ferrying Division's foreign transport service, General Tunner organized a fleet of aircraft specifically dedicated to the air evacuation mission. This allowed for safe evacuation of wounded soldiers to rear areas where they could receive better medical care. During one month, this service successfully evacuated 3,480 patients.[65] His superiors summed up that "General Tunner's well-formed plans for Air Evacuation may well serve as a model for the movement of patients from the battlefronts to domestic hospitals, resulting in consequent saving of time and soldiers' lives."[66]

The ferrying of aircraft and the air transport mission are not typically viewed with the same interest as air-to-air dogfights and large bombing raids. Nonetheless, the Ferrying Division's contributions were critical to the American war effort. Tunner's success accomplishing the ferrying mission led to greater responsibility, additional command opportunities, and a more direct role in the war.

Notes

1. Dobson, *US Wartime Aid to Britain*, 31.
2. Ibid., 30.
3. "Chapter 1, The Establishment of the Ferrying Command," 15.
4. Appendix, "Office of the Chief of the Air Corps, For the Assistant Secretary of War for Air," 298.

5. "Chapter 1, The Establishment of the Ferrying Command," 19.

6. LeMay, oral history interview, 1–2.

7. Appendix, "Office of the Chief of the Air Corps, For the Assistant Secretary of War for Air," 298.

8. Appendix, Col Robert Olds, Commander, Air Corps Ferrying Command, 329.

9. Tunner, *Over the Hump*, 21.

10. "Chapter 5, Operations of the Ferrying Command, June to December 1941," 251–52.

11. Air Corps Ferrying Command, "Operating Instruction," 2.

12. Tunner, oral history interview, 27.

13. Appendix, War Department Circular 55–20, 334–35.

14. Air Corps Ferrying Command, "Operating Instruction," 1.

15. Ibid., 9.

16. Tunner, *Over the Hump*, 21.

17. Ibid., 22.

18. Ibid.

19. Ibid., 23.

20. Air Transport Command, *The Origins of the Ferrying Division*, vol. 1, 130.

21. Tunner, *Over the Hump*, 25.

22. Appendix: "Organization of the Air Corp Ferrying Command," 802.

23. Air Transport Command, *The Origins of the Ferrying Division*, vol. 2, 437.

24. Ibid., 433.

25. Ibid., 551.

26. Ibid., 553.

27. Ibid., 579.

28. Appendix, Lt Col William H. Tunner, Commander, Domestic Division.

29. 2nd Ferrying Group History, 7.

30. "Chapter 8, Headquarters and other Organizational Developments, Spring 1942, the Domestic Wing, the Groups: Personnel Problems 2," 591–92.

31. 2nd Ferrying Group History, 7; and "Chapter 8, Headquarters and other Organizational Developments, Spring 1942, the Domestic Wing, the Groups: Personnel Problems 2," 593.

32. "Chapter 8, Headquarters and other Organizational Developments, Spring 1942, the Domestic Wing, the Groups: Personnel Problems 2," 603.

33. Ibid., 575.

34. Ibid., 610–11.

35. Ibid., 612–13.

36. Ibid., 615–16.

37. Ibid., 701.

38. Ibid., 704–06.

39. Ibid., 915.

40. Air Transport Command, *The Origins of the Ferrying Division*, vol. 3, 3.

41. Ibid., 30.

42. Exerpt from Ferry Tales Newspaper, "Ferrying Division Trains Pilots and Crew Members for Many Missions," March 1945, 2nd Ferrying Group History, 52.

43. Tunner, *Over the Hump*, 26–7.

44. 2nd Ferrying Group History, 51. Training aircraft included: BC-1A, UC-78, A-25, C-60, Hudson RA-414, C-73, P-47, AT-9, B-25, B-26, B-24, and B-17.

45. Ibid., 51–2.

46. Air Transport Command, *The Origins of the Ferrying Division*, vol. 3, 79.

47. Ibid., vol. 2, 714.

48. Tunner, *Over the Hump*, 29.

49. Ibid., 42.

50. Appendix, Col William H. Tunner, 237.

51. Memorandum, "To: Commanding General, Army Air Forces."

52. Air Transport Command, The Origins of the Ferrying Division, vol. 3, 70.

53. Ibid., 65.

54. 2nd Ferrying Group History, 103.

55. Ibid., 105.

56. Tunner, oral history interview, 32.

57. Air Transport Command, *The Origins of the Ferrying Division*, vol. 2, 723–25.

58. Ibid., 723.

59. Tunner, *Over the Hump*, 39.

60. Air Transport Command, Memorandum, "To Commanding General, Army Air Forces."

61. Tunner, *Over the Hump*, 39.

62. Air Transport Command, Memorandum, "Recommendation for award."

63. Tunner, *Over the Hump*, 39–40.

64. Ibid., 40.

65. "Report of Decorations Board."

66. Air Transport Command, Memorandum, "Recommendation for award," 1.

Chapter 4

Leadership Actions
The Hump Airlift Operation

I was fully aware, as I increased military discipline, cleanliness and courtesy, and ordered parades and inspections on Saturdays, that I might be jeopardizing any chance of winning a popularity contest. This did not bother me a bit; I was not there to be a good fellow, but to get results. I had already become known as a cold, hard driver, with the nickname "Willie the Whip" whispered behind my back, and I didn't lose any sleep over it.

—Lt Gen William H. Tunner

While the United States emphasized aiding Great Britain and winning the war in Europe, there also existed a strong though lesser commitment to supporting China's struggle against the Japanese Imperial Army.[1] Prior to the United States' entry into World War II, this aid came primarily from Lend-Lease supplies and materials and from a group of rowdy pilots of the American Volunteer Group (AVG), called the "Flying Tigers," commanded by Brig Gen Claire L. Chennault.[2]

In February 1942, providing support to Allied forces in China became more complicated when the Japanese invaded Burma and cut off the remaining ground supply routes from India to China. While this Japanese victory was a blow to the Allied war effort in the Pacific, President Roosevelt remained committed to China: "I want to say to the gallant people of China that no matter what advances the Japanese may make, ways will be found to deliver airplanes and munitions to the armies of China. We remember that the Chinese people were the first to stand up and fight against the aggressors in this war."[3] With China now isolated by land and sea, the president turned to General Arnold and the Air Corps to establish air supply routes from India to China, which became known as the "Hump" routes due to the 16,000-foot-high Himalaya Mountains the airplanes

27

had to clear. In April 1942, the United States began the Hump airlift operation.

Tunner summed up the initial effort saying, "During April and May, under command of the 10th Air Force, a handful of planes, mostly C-47's, flew a total of 308 tons to China. By August the monthly figure had reached 700 tons, but this was certainly not going to keep the Chinese in the war."[4] While reports from the theater blamed these results on insufficient aircraft, maintenance, and personnel support, it also became apparent that the 10th Air Force was not the proper organization to be running the air transport mission.

Brig Gen Cyrus Smith, deputy commander of the Air Transport Command, proposed that ATC take over the mission. As Smith put it, "The principal experience of the Air Transport Command is in air transportation, as contrasted with the experience of the theater commander being principally in combat and in preparation for combat. . . . The India-China Ferry operation must be conducted on the best standards of transportation if it is to have maximum effectiveness."[5] The Air Transport Command took over control of the Hump airlift on 1 December 1942 and shifted additional assets to the operation. In February 1943, the ATC airlift successfully transported 2,855 tons to China.[6]

Throughout 1943, the Hump airlift requirements grew under pressure from the Chinese government and General Chennault's desire for an aggressive air campaign against the Japanese in China. As a result, the president ordered ATC to increase Hump airlift tonnage to a minimum of 7,000 tons in July and 10,000 in September and each month thereafter.[7] General Arnold committed additional aircraft and personnel to the operation, and by December 1943, the airlift was meeting the president's goal of at least 10,000 tons per month. However, these hard-won increases came at a heavy cost. During the last half of 1943, there were 153 major aircraft accidents and 168 crew fatalities on the Hump route.[8] According to General Smith, "We are paying for it [increased tonnage over the Hump] in men and planes."[9] Both tonnage and accidents increased into 1944. It was in this context that General Tunner took charge of the Hump airlift.

When now General George assigned Tunner to command the India-China Division (ICD) of ATC, he explained the problems there as twofold: "First, in accordance with the commitment made by the President of the United States to our Allies, we must raise the tonnage that we are airlifting to China. Second, we must cut down on our accident rate. We're losing too many crews, too many planes."[10]

Prior to taking command, Tunner and a small staff visited the region to learn what they faced. Tunner commandeered an aircraft and flew one of the Hump air routes himself. He also toured the run-down base facilities and talked with flyers and maintainers to gauge their wellbeing. "Mountains and jungles, Japanese and head-hunters, storms and icing, mosquitoes and filth—I had no picnic ahead of me, that was sure. And yet, when I reported in to General George after my trip . . . I was confident that we could fulfill the double mission of increasing tonnage and decreasing accidents."[11]

Increasing Tonnage

When General Tunner took command in August 1944, he understood the "responsibilities a military leader gathers when he tries to do the job he was sent out to do. He often finds he has to handle the incidentals first, before he can even get on with the primary task."[12] From his early trip to India, Tunner recognized that the difficult living and operating conditions were hurting morale and professionalism. There was unbearable heat, monsoon rains, and a variety of insects that infested every bunk.[13] The men resembled their environment and tended to be poorly groomed and dressed, with few showing any sign of common courtesy, much less military courtesy. Tunner realized that "in this unhappy and unclean environment lived the mechanics to whose maintenance were entrusted the lives of our fliers, the supply men whose job was to keep spare parts on hand and available, and all the other members of that huge complex necessary to keep planes flying—and flying safely."[14]

Tunner began by ordering that all living and operating areas be cleaned and inspected on a regular basis. He coordinated the use of stripped-down B-25s for insect spraying and malaria prevention.[15] The bulk of Tunner's push was intended to bring military discipline and all that it entailed to the ICD.

29

> I just told them to put out the orders and said we would carry on these military activities from now on. We would become a military organization; we would have saluting; we would have 'yes sir' and 'no sir;' we would have parades and inspections on Saturday just like any other military organization. . . . We had good parades and inspections and the whole place started to bloom. People wanted, basically, to be proud of the Army, proud of the Air Corps. They wanted to be proud of their job.[16]

When morale picked up, Tunner was not surprised. "I was by no means unaware that a positive result of this new-found cleanliness, pride, and patriotism might well result in increased efficiency and performance. I have been taught . . . bases that were well run, clean, orderly and soldierly did a better operating job."[17]

With standards set and a foundation for discipline in place, General Tunner and his staff addressed the primary tasks of increasing tonnage and decreasing accidents. He stressed that increasing airlift production must be balanced against operating safely. In early 1945, Tunner emphasized to his base commanders that "in striving for high aircraft utilization, we will *not* sacrifice flying safety. One hour of daily utilization lost can be made up later . . . the loss of one load of passengers and crew can never be recovered [emphasis in original]."[18] General Tunner and his staff therefore pushed for improvements in training, maintenance, and operations.

General Tunner initiated two training programs that were designed to familiarize aircrews with dangers of the Hump. New pilots in the ICD were required to undertake a four-phase course that included preflight inspection instruction, ground Link trainer practice, local area flights, and en route training.[19] Each of these phases culminated in evaluations. Tunner's second program addressed a common fear among aircrew—having to crash-land or bail out over the jungle. "The only way I could see to dispel this fear was to strip the jungle of its secrets. I ordered each base to establish a jungle indoctrination camp, in which our men could see and explore the jungle themselves, under the guidance of trained jungle scouts."[20] These camps were based on the theory that "jungle knowledge is best acquired by living in the jungle—making the acquaintance of jungle people, becoming familiar with various types of jungle terrain, and subsisting partly on the fare which can be found in the jungle by those who know how."[21] Together, these training improvements provided aircrews the opportunity to gain experience and confidence prior to flying missions.

Drawing upon his previous experience in air transportation, Tunner emphasized the importance of efficient maintenance operations within his command. "I constantly inspected the maintenance operations, probably devoting more time to this activity than to any other. I was no expert, but I could recognize efficiency and results."[22] Maintenance operations had been a sore spot in Hump airlift operations. Maintenance crew chiefs were assigned to a single aircraft. If their aircraft was flying or did not have any problems, they would often disappear from the flight line. To increase efficiency, Tunner adopted a process similar to the production lines in US automobile factories. As outlined in table 2, production-line maintenance (PLM) provided a sequence of work stations that each aircraft would proceed through. Tunner elaborated that "when airplanes came in and they needed their 200-hour inspection, or their 50-hour inspections, they would take a place in the line at the end of the line and every 3 hours, or every 6 hours, they'd move up a notch."[23] Assigning maintainers to the various stages allowed for efficient use of division personnel. Tunner credited PLM with increasing aircraft utilization rates, reducing the time required for maintenance work, and improving the quality of maintenance inspections.[24]

Table 2. Hump airlift production-line maintenance sequence

Maintenance Station	Work Scheduled
Station No. 1	Initial engine run-up; general inspection of airplane and its forms; work planning
Station No. 2	Airplane wash and polish, inside and out; cowlings removed, engines sprayed and cleaned; sumps drained, etc.
Station No. 3	Carburetion; communications; propellers and anti-icer system
Station No. 4	Power plant, ignition system (removal of plugs), lubricating system, power section, accessory section, engine controls; oxygen system; painting of placards and insignia; rigging and surface controls
Station No. 5	Instruments; automatic pilot; electrical system, engine section, fuselage section, cockpit section; hydraulic system, landing gear (including retraction); wheels and brakes, tires; de-icer system; general lubrication
Station No. 6	Final inspection; replacement of operational equipment
Station No. 7	Preflight, final run-up, servicing

Adapted from Tunner, *Over the Hump*, 94.

31

In addition to improving training and maintenance programs, Tunner relentlessly expanded the airlift. He believed that he could quickly exceed the Air Corp's August 1944 target of 13,000 tons delivered, reporting that he could produce 20,500 tons in October, 27,500 in November, and 31,000 in December. However, this was contingent upon increasing the number of airfields, aircraft, and personnel available to his command.[25] He was successful in all areas. In July of 1944, the ICD was operating from six airfields in India into six airfields in China. By the end of the operation in November 1945, the division had expanded to operating 25 air routes between 13 airfields in India and 10 in China (see figure 3).[26]

The Hump operation inreased its number of airplanes significantly in early 1945. In December 1944, the average number of aircraft in service was 249.6; in January 1945, it was 287.4; in February, 336.8; in April, 325.9; and in July, 332. Personnel strength also grew. At Hump locations in India, the number of

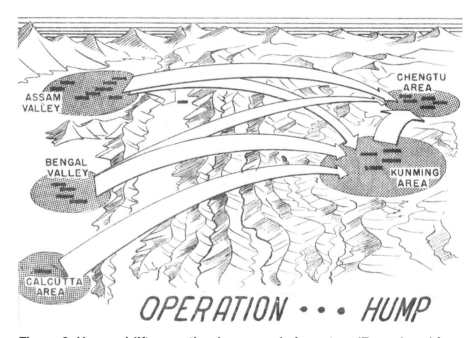

Figure 3. Hump airlift operating bases and air routes. (Reproduced from Task Force Times, "Hump and Lift," 26 March 1949, 2, in Combined Airlift Task Force, History, vol. 2, 572.02 V. 2, March 1949, 00241455, AFHRA.)

workers rose from 19,025 in January to 22,359 by midyear.[27] Tunner used the local population for labor and by January 1945 had hired approximately 25,000 civilians as mechanics, welders, painters, smiths, and other specialties.[28]

By improving and expanding operations, Tunner was able to run what was described as "Big Business in the Air" and meet his vision for the airlift.

> Our operating policy was that each plane must be flying, be undergoing maintenance, or be in the process of loading or unloading every second of every day . . . We did not fly schedules on the Hump; rather, each plane proceeded automatically and immediately from each function to the next. When its time came for maintenance, it went to the shop, and when it was ready for flight, it was loaded and then took off. That went on day and night. This is how you build up tonnage, by the constant utilization of equipment.[29]

Reducing Accidents

As commanding general of the ICD, Tunner's second assigned mission was to reduce the high accident rate associated with the airlift. The beginning of the Hump had seen many lives and aircraft lost. Bad weather, air traffic congestion, and young crews made flying dangerous.[30] In January 1944, for every 218 flights over the Hump, one airplane was lost. For every 1,000 tons transported to China, 2.94 lives were lost. This meant an astounding one American life for every 340 tons.[31] Although increasing tonnage while decreasing accidents was daunting, Tunner applied his previous experience with flight safety. He expressed that "accidents were predictable, therefore preventable. Thus the mission of flying safety was to anticipate and promptly correct conditions leading to events which would cause accidents."[32] With this approach, Tunner and his staff instituted procedures and programs designed to influence behavior and improve safety.

Tunner's staff surgeon identified part of the safety problem, reporting that "fifty per cent of the crew members are bordering on a frank operational fatigue. Several recent accidents are directly attributable to flying fatigue."[33] The rotation policy contributed to the problem, stating that when a pilot reached 650 flying hours he would be allowed to rotate back to the States. This resulted in pilots flying as much as they could in order to leave as soon as possible. Tunner instituted a new rotation policy that required both a minimum number of hours flown in support of Hump operations and a minimum of one year served with ICD.[34] In announcing this policy to his aircrews, Tunner stated, "It is imperative that we relieve our crews of their present tension of the pressure to build up maximum hours in minimum time. The longer periods of service are not only to the benefit of the crew members, themselves, but to promote more complete utilization of flying skill, a better flying safety record, and altogether, a more efficient operation."[35] The accident rate declined.

The flying safety program was a priority for Tunner and his staff, focusing on four areas:

1. Investigation and analysis of existing flight and maintenance procedures and practices

2. Statistical analysis of accidents

3. Recommendations for correcting faults

4. Prompt action and follow-up

The safety program included: crew briefings, flight planning, aircraft cargo loading, en route weather, navigation, communication, and aircrew procedural discipline.[36]

Weather was a consistent problem for crews flying the Hump. As one pilot described, "Winds up to 125 m.p.h. swept the mountain peaks. Violent rain, snow, and hail storms knocked out astrodomes and caused other aircraft damage. Severe icing conditions forced some crews to jettison cargo. Radio contact with ground installations was impossible and some navigation instruments froze tight."[37] Through investigation and analysis, Tunner became convinced that "weather on the Hump was a major accident factor," and stated that "when a pilot flew into a particularly severe storm, found his plane being buffeted around and icing up to the extent that he just might not make it, that man had my orders to turn around and come back."[38] While Tunner's emphasis on flight safety may have reduced tonnage during April 1945, it likely led to the sharp decrease in accidents for the remainder of the operation.[39]

With tonnage rising and accidents decreasing, Tunner's initiatives were producing positive results not only within the ICD but throughout the theater. From 21 April to 11 May 1945, ICD conducted Operation Rooster, transporting the Chinese 6th Army to Kunming to assist in the defense of the 14th Air Force (successor to the AVG Flying Tigers) base at Chihkiang. ICD flew 1,648 trips, hauling 25,136 troops, 2,178 horses, and 1,565 tons of materials, for a total of 5,523 tons. In addition, 369 tons of aviation gasoline were flown to Chihkiang for 14th Air Force fighters.[40]

The ICD also received praise for its support of the Operation Matterhorn B-29s. XX Bomber Command of 20th Air Force attacked Japanese targets from austere bases in China. Brig Gen Joseph Smith, chief of staff, XX Bomber Command, wrote General Tunner that "there were many times when the success or failure of the missions of the XX Bomber Command depended upon the delivery of gasoline and supplies during extremely bad weather. Not once during our year of operation were our missions curtailed because of the lack of supplies due to the timely help given by the members of your splendid organization, often entailing efforts of your personnel far beyond their normal duties."[41] Maj Gen Clayton Bissell, commanding general, 10th Air Force, similarly recognized the ICD stating that "the Burma and China campaigns have been financed entirely by air, and one of the largest military machines on earth has had its only outside support through the medium of air transport."[42]

On 1 August 1945, to celebrate Army Air Forces Day, the ICD transported 5,237 tons of freight to China and made a total of 1,118 trips within a period of 24 hours.[43] According to Tunner, "Nothing like this had ever been done on the command scale before. Though we kept going at full throttle for the full twenty-four hours—I don't think anybody slept—there was a camaraderie and a spirit that made it more fun than work."[44] He went on to say that "perhaps the most heart-warming result of the big day to me was the accident rate. It was zero. In all that flying, and flying under pressure, there was not one single accident."[45] Table 3 illustrates General Tunner's success in leading the ICD and prosecuting the Hump airlift operation. According to the official Air Force history of World War II, "Air Transport Command's crowded airways to China were the proving ground, if not the birthplace, of mass strategic airlift. Here the AAF [Army Air Forces] demonstrated conclusively that a vast quantity of cargo could be delivered by air, even under the most unfavorable circumstances."[46]

Table 3. Increased tonnage and reduced accidents

1944	Hump Lift India to China	Accident Rate per Thousand Hours
September	22,314 tons	.682
October	24,715	.478
November	34,914	.445
December	31,935	.571
1945		
January	44,098	.301
February	40,677	.497
March	46,545	.580
April	44,254	.511
May	46,393	.372
June	55,386	.323
July	71,042	.358
August	53,315	.239

Adapted from Wesley Frank Craven and James Lea Cate, *The Army Air Forces in World War II*, vol. 7, *Services Around the World* (Washington, DC: Office of Air Force History, 1953), 138 and 143; and 1306th Army Air Forces Base Unit, India Wing, India China Division, Air Transport Command, Office of the Intelligence and Security Officer. "Special Intelligence Report, 13 September 1945, an attachment to United States Air Forces in Europe, "Karache [sic.] Investigation, End of War," 168.7158-278, 1945, 01096945. AFHRA. Roll 3016, frames 311-323.

A New Mission

Following Japan's surrender on 15 August, the ICD reduced the number of flights over the Hump and brought the airlift operation to a close at the end of November 1945. Tunner met with US theater commanders based in India and China to talk about a plan that he and his staff had been discussing for many weeks. He recommended "the establishment of postwar ATC routes in order to pave the way for eventual American air transport commercial lines."[47] Supported by the theater commanders and General George, this effort became known as the Orient Project. Tunner said that with "50 of our C-54s and 5,000 men who were all volunteers, we could keep them over there and start an airline in this great vacuum of air transportation and eventually turn it over to some American airline."[48] This would turn out to be easier said than done.

While securing the aircraft seemed possible, finding volunteers proved more challenging. The volunteer issue came to a boil in a congressional report about a postwar visit with ICD troops:

> I'll tell you what ATC is doing here. You can see it clearly from this request for 5,000 enlisted men and 700 officers to volunteer to stay here another year. ATC is here to build up private airline services. Private airlines cannot get a franchise here, but the government can. So they want you to stay and work for a private concern at Army pay!. . .What followed these remarks (from an NCO) was not applause, but a demonstration—whistling, cheering, stamping, shouts, indicating that this man had summed up everyone's fears.[49]

Tunner's personal life unexpectedly complicated the Orient Project. "My wife had come down with a very serious cancer, brain cancer, and I was told to come back to the States. I went back and stayed there for a couple of days . . . then I went back to India. Sometime later I was sent another wire saying that she was going to be operated on and I had better come home and stay home this time."[50] With Tunner's departure, the Orient Project quickly fell apart and was terminated. His wife would die a year and a half later.

Tunner believed that the Orient Project collapsed because "the boss had run out on his own project, and those who had volunteered lost faith. I am positive that had I been able to remain in India, I could have held the project together long enough for some airline to take over."[51] "Personally, I was plunged from the peak of accomplishment and the glory of success to the depths of grief and the despair of failure. I still do not know how I could possibly have taken any different course of action, but I do know that my leaving Asia meant the death knell of the Orient Project."[52] It is difficult to determine if Tunner's grief and despair resulted from the death of his wife or the failure of his mission. While this period was a low point in Tunner's life, he would continue to champion the air transport element of airpower and would soon find himself leading the first major battle of the Cold War.

37

Notes

1. Craven and Cate, *The Army Air Forces in World War II*, vol. 5, 13–14.
2. Scott, Rainey, and Hunt, *The Logistics of War*, 110.
3. Ibid.
4. Tunner, *Over the Hump*, 60.
5. Ibid., 61.
6. Craven and Cate, *The Army Air Forces in World War II*, vol. 7, 123.
7. Ibid., 125.
8. Scott, Rainey, and Hunt, *The Logistics of War*, 112.
9. Ibid.
10. Tunner, *Over the Hump*, 52.
11. Ibid., 85.
12. Ibid., 86.
13. Scott, Rainey, and Hunt, *The Logistics of War*, 111.
14. Tunner, *Over the Hump*, 57.
15. 2nd Ferrying Group History, 236.
16. Tunner, oral history interview, 27.
17. Tunner, *Over the Hump*, 91.
18. Craven and Cate, *Army Air Forces in World War II*, vol. 7, 142 (emphasis in original).
19. India-China Division (ICD), "Arriving Pilots." A Link trainer is an early version of a flight simulator where pilots could practice cockpit and instrument flight procedures.
20. Tunner, *Over the Hump*, 100.
21. ICD, "Kemi-Nodi Sojourners Learn."
22. Tunner, *Over the Hump*, 93–94.
23. Tunner, oral history interview, 46–48.
24. Craven and Cate, *Army Air Forces in World War II*, vol. 7, 141.
25. Ibid., 138.
26. "Hump and Lift," *The Task Force Times*, 2.
27. Craven and Cate, *Army Air Forces in World War II*, vol. 7, 141.
28. CD, "Division is Big Employer."
29. Tunner, *Over the Hump*, 118.
30. Air Transport Command, Memorandum, 3.
31. La Farge, *The Eagle in the Egg*, 125.
32. Tunner, *Over the Hump*, 102.
33. Ibid., 90.
34. Austin, Memorandum.
35. ICD, "New Policy for Rotation."
36. Tunner, *Over the Hump*, 102.
37. ICD, "Hump's Worst Weather." An astrodome is a transparent dome on the top of an aircraft through which celestial observations are made for navigation.
38. Tunner, *Over the Hump*, 113.
39. Craven and Cate, *Army Air Forces in World War II*, vol. 7, 143. Just over 44,000 tons were flown versus 48,000 that were forecast.
40. Ibid., 149.

41. Brig Gen Joseph Smith, 20th Air Force, Office of Deputy Command.

42. Maj Gen Clayton Bissel, Military Intelligence Division, Office of the Chief of Staff, letter.

43. Army Air Forces, India Burma Theater, Memorandum.

44. Tunner, *Over the Hump*, 133.

45. Ibid., 134.

46. Craven and Cate, *Army Air Forces in World War II*, vol. 7, 151.

47. Tunner, *Over the Hump*, 138.

48. Tunner, oral history interview, 66.

49. Office of the Intelligence and Security Officer, 1306th Army Air Forces Base Unit, 5–6.

50. Tunner, oral history interview, 67.

51. Tunner, *Over the Hump*, 149.

52. Ibid., 151.

Chapter 5

Leadership Actions
The Berlin Airlift

In a successful airlift you don't see planes parked all over the place; they're either in the air, on loading or unloading ramps, or being worked on. You don't see personnel milling around; flying crews are either flying, or resting up so that they can fly again tomorrow. Ground crews are either working on their assigned planes, or resting up so that they can work on them again tomorrow. Everyone else is also on the job, going about his work quietly and efficiently.

—Lt Gen William H. Tunner

From the beginning of World War II, President Roosevelt and his advisors were certain that postwar peace was sustainable only through the cooperation of the Soviet Union, the United States, and Great Britain. The president wanted these states to operate as policemen in reestablishing society, and he was convinced by its collaboration during the war that the Soviet Union would cooperate after the war.[1] Before invading Germany, the United States, Britain, and the Soviet Union formed an occupation commission. It was agreed that the Allies would divide Germany into three zones: the Soviets occupying the east, the British in the northwest, and the Americans in the southwest.[2] While Berlin fell into the Soviet occupation zone, it was agreed that the city would be divided into sectors garrisoned and administered by the military forces of the Allied powers. This decision to divide the city would provide the basis for the Berlin crisis of 1948.[3]

The Soviets were first into Berlin and made efforts to solidify their position. Even while they were still wreaking havoc, the Soviets began a campaign to misinform the Germans and convince them that they alone had saved the city from Nazi control.[4] While these actions focused on establishing a dominant position in Berlin, Soviet Secretary General Joseph Stalin, also had a long-range goal for the city of Berlin and for all of Germany. On

4 June 1945, Stalin told a group of German communist leaders that Germany would remain divided for a time. He explained that his plan was to establish Soviet authority in the eastern occupation zone and then weaken the British in their region. He expected the United States to withdraw within two years and believed Germany would unite under communist control within the Soviet orbit.[5]

Starting in January 1948, and combined with other aggressive political and economic actions, the Soviets began a gradual campaign to disrupt transportation and communication between the western zones and Berlin. US and British rail, road, and barge transportation were the targets of detailed passenger and cargo inspections, unexplained detours and delays, and shutdowns in service due to "safety issues" and repairs.[6] When the Americans and the British challenged the Soviets on the legality of restricting access to Berlin, they were surprised to find that no written agreement secured this right. During the confusion at the end of the war, western policymakers failed to establish guaranteed access to Berlin by surface transportation.[7] The full Soviet blockade of Berlin began on 24 June, and was explained in the following message:

> Transportation Division of the Soviet Military Administration is compelled to halt all passenger and freight traffic to and from Berlin tomorrow at 0600 hours because of technical difficulties. . . . It is impossible to reroute traffic in the interests of maintaining rail service, since such measures would unfavorably affect the entire railroad traffic in the Soviet Occupation Zone . . . water traffic will also be suspended. . . . Coal shipments to Berlin from the Soviet authorities have also ordered the central switching stations to stop the supply of electrical power from the Soviet Zone and Soviet Sector to the Western sectors. Shortage of coal to operate the plants and technical difficulties . . . are the reasons.[8]

While the blockade disrupted surface transportation into Berlin, it did not cut off every means of supporting the city.

Unlike surface transportation, a written agreement between the Soviet Union and the Western Allies covered air transportation. In November 1945, the Allies established three 20-mile-wide air corridors between the western occupation zones and Berlin to help deconflict US and British air traffic from Soviet aircraft operating within the eastern zone.[9] Based on their lack of air transport experience and their familiarity with the failed German airlift at Stalingrad, the Soviets did not expect a western airlift.[10]

The Western Allies considered a variety of responses to the harassment and the blockade of Berlin, ranging from withdrawal to armed conflict. They decided to support Berlin from the air. Pres. Harry S. Truman made it clear that all necessary resources were to be allocated to form the needed airlift organization.[11] Initially, the US airlift would focus on supporting the American occupation forces, a mission that would require lifting 500 to 700 tons a day for three to four weeks. This task would fall to Lt Gen Curtis LeMay, commander of US Air Forces in Europe (USAFE), who designated Brig Gen Joseph Smith to supervise the operation.[12] The British airlift effort began with similar goals and timelines and was known as Operation Plainfare.

The American airlift began on 26 June, with 32 C-47 flights transporting 80 tons of supplies to Berlin.[13] On 29 June, the airlift expanded to support the entire population in the western sectors of Berlin by insuring that the most flights possible were flown and that the best operational efficiency was preserved.[14] General Smith rapidly assembled an airlift fleet of 102 C-47s and 54 C-54s, and after three weeks of flying, Operation Vittles was transporting over 1,500 tons a day.[15] However, the crews were inexperienced in managing a transport service and the leadership knew little concerning the organizing of an airlift. Thus, the early stages of the operations were not well structured.

From his desk in Washington, General Tunner, now the MATS deputy commander, could tell that the airlift could stand improvement.

> To any of us familiar with the airlift business, some of the features of Operation Vittles which were most enthusiastically reported by the press were contradictions of efficient administration. Pilots were flying twice as many hours per week as they should, for example; newspaper stories told of the way they continued on, though exhausted. I read how desk officers took off whenever they got a chance and ran to the flight line to find planes sitting there waiting for them. This was all very exciting, and loads of fun, but successful operations are not built on such methods.[16]

He later described the early days of the airlift stating, "It was a mistake to put a man in a learning position when things were so hot. Joe Smith was a good man and, of course, LeMay was a good man. But they didn't know air transportation . . . it was booming, but it was about to fall apart."[17] On 26 July 1948, General Tunner brought his expertise in air transportation to the Berlin airlift.

Tunner stated that the airlift operation "deserved the same practices and techniques, the same standards . . . and the proven rigidity in flying procedures and flying safety that we had developed in India."[18] When assigned to command the airlift (see figure 4), he moved quickly to secure his staff of experts and position his airlift organization for success. He pulled many of his "old reliables" from the Hump to fill positions in operations, maintenance, air traffic control, communications, supply, and airdrome construction.[19] Tunner realized that proven airlift practices and a staff of air transport experts would provide an essential foundation for the Berlin airlift.

Initially tasked with maximizing sorties and efficiency, Tunner set out to evaluate his new command. On his first inspection trip to Berlin, Tunner noted that "there was much milling around of flight personnel. Crews left their planes while they were being

Figure 4. Brigadier General Tunner—Commander, Airlift Task Force. (Reproduced from an Air Force photograph, http://www.af.mil/shared/media/ photodb/photos/040315-F-9999G-027.jpg.)

44

unloaded to smoke, lounge, and gossip in a snack bar. When the planes were ready for takeoff on their return trips the crews frequently were not."[20] Tunner ordered that aircrews were not to leave their aircraft during turnaround. Upon landing, an operations officer and a weatherman would drive out to each aircraft to advise the pilots on information pertaining to their return trip. In addition, a snack truck would come to the plane to provide food and drinks for the crews. As a result, turnaround time was reduced to 30 minutes.[21]

On 10 August, Tunner's mission was altered to reflect the growing needs in Berlin's western sectors. The official mission orders specified that the goal of the British and American units be a total of 4,500 tons per day.[22]

Weather was a major obstacle. On 13 August 1948, known as "Black Friday," Tunner was flying an airlift mission to Berlin, as reported below:

> As Tunner's airplane neared Berlin, the weather grew worse. Clouds dropped to the tops of buildings, sheets of rain obscured radar, and everything generally "went to hell." One C-54 missed the runway, crashed, and burned; a second landed and blew its main tires when the heavily loaded aircraft avoided hitting the wreck; a third missed the main strip entirely and ground-looped on an auxiliary runway. Aircraft began stacking. . . . Soon a huge, confusing, milling mass of aircraft circled in a stack from 3,000 to 12,000 feet in danger of collision or of drifting out of the corridors completely.[23]

From his aircraft, Tunner took charge, ordering the air traffic controller to "send everybody in the stack below and above me home. Then tell me when it's O.K. to come down."[24] Tunner and his staff instituted procedures to improve efficiency and prevent many of the problems encountered on Black Friday.

Tunner began by establishing a standard set of flight rules and procedures to govern airlift operations. He decreed that all planes under his command would "fly a never-changing flight pattern by instrument rules at all times, good weather or bad, night or day."[25] Pilots flying the new procedures followed a set route that required great precision. A series of set headings, climb rates, altitudes, airspeeds, and radio calls were flown from takeoff through landing in Berlin.[26]

To avoid the problem of stacking aircraft over the airfield, crews were restricted to a single landing attempt in Berlin. According to Tunner, "We set up a system where by each airplane would come down to levels which were prescribed for that field . . . if you can see the field you land; if you can't, shove forward your throttles and turn on the course for home and go back home."[27] To emphasize these procedures, and perhaps indicating his frustration with Black Friday, Tunner threatened "to reduce any pilot to copilot status who did not land with ceiling and visibility greater than 400 feet and a mile and to court-martial any pilot who did land with ceiling and visibility of less than 400 feet and a mile."[28] These procedures resulted in what Tunner viewed as a "conveyor belt," (see figure 5) where aircraft would consistently takeoff, fly, and land at three-minute intervals, every hour of every day (see figure 6).[29]

Figure 5. C-54 aircraft lined up for unloading. (Reproduced from Combined Airlift Task Force, History, "Photos of the Berlin Air Lift, 572.08, July–August 1948, 00241465, AFHRA.")

Following the implementation of the new flight rules and procedures, General Tunner organized a meeting with 30 of his pilots to get their perspectives on the airlift. Over beer and cold cuts, Tunner spent more than nine hours listening to their issues, which ranged from ways to improve flight rules to poor living conditions. Tunner made some changes on the spot, and his staff fixed several of the issues within a few days.[30]

Tunner was known for wandering around the airlift operation. "Night and day, wearing an old olive-green flight jacket stripped of rank badges, a baseball cap crammed on his head, he shuttled from Wiesbaden to Tempelhof to Fassberg and back, grabbing coffee and doughnuts where he could."[31] According to Tunner,

> I would purposely pick late at night or the very early morning hours to check up on what I considered important or vital activities. It wasn't unusual for a sleepy tower operator to suddenly realize that I was standing there with him. Sometimes there would be no conversation other than a greeting or a good night; there wasn't much need for words when things were going properly. The word got around that the General had been there during the small hours. It was a twenty-four-hour operation everyday, and I wanted everyone in the Airlift to remember that.[32]

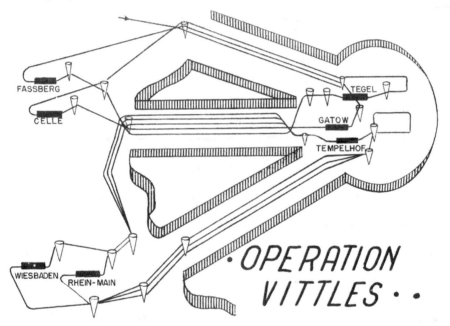

Figure 6. Berlin airlift operating bases and air-route structure. (Reproduced from Task Force Times, "Hump and Lift," 26 March 1949, 2, in Combined Airlift Task Force, History, vol. 2, 572.02 V. 2, March 1949, 00241455, AFHRA.)

For Tunner, airlift efficiency and problem solving extended beyond the flight line. When airlift pilots began complaining about sluggish aircraft performance, Tunner immediately looked into the problem. "We went down to the yards where the coal was loaded and found that there was great carelessness on the part of the Army, who was responsible for having the bags of coal loaded and that some bags which were supposed to weigh 100 pounds would be 120 or 80, but we got uniformity in that. We had everything carefully weighed before we loaded, so we didn't overload airplanes. . . . Things of that type are what a transport man knows [see figures 7 and 8]."[33] The airlift later established a weights-and-balance program.[34]

General Tunner pushed a spirit of competition within his command. He consistently encouraged his squadrons and bases to try new procedures for increasing efficiency and tonnage. "Howgozit" charts were displayed in every squadron to inform the men of their performance compared to other units.[35] These statistics were also published in the airlift's daily newspaper, *The Task Force Times.*

He challenged his organization to exceed expectations. "Our first big day was Air Force Day, 18 September, when we emulated

Figure 7. C-54 aircraft being loaded. (Reproduced from Combined Airlift Task Force, History, "Photos of the Berlin Air Lift, 572.08, July–August 1948, 00241465, AFHRA.")

Figure 8. C-54 aircraft being loaded. (Reproduced from Combined Airlift Task Force, History, "Photos of the Berlin Air Lift, 572.08, July–August 1948, 00241465, AFHRA.")

our successful celebration of that day on the Hump three years before and set out to break records. We airlifted a total tonnage of 5,582 tons to Berlin in the twenty-four-hour period. The British added 1,400 tons, for a total of nearly 7,000 tons. It was one of those all-out, enthusiastic efforts that permeated the entire command. It gave us all a booster shot of enthusiasm, and the daily tonnage stayed high."[36] The airlift was meeting its assigned goal of averaging 4,500 tons a day, but Tunner's mission and the organization were about to change.

Tunner realized that the operation would function "much more smoothly and efficiently if the British and American operations were combined."[37] Tunner saw several advantages of a combined operation, including the consolidation of scheduled flights, expanded basing of American aircraft in the British zone, and increased utilization of the two northern corridors. By using the bigger American planes on shorter routes, Tunner could increase efficiency and tonnage. For example, "two C-54s operating from the English bases were equal to nine twin engine planes operating from the American bases."[38] Tunner presented this idea to General LeMay, who coordinated with his British counterpart to establish the Combined Airlift Task Force (CALTF).

In an order dated 15 October 1948, Major General Tunner became CALTF commander, with Air Commodore J. W. F. Merer assigned as his deputy. CALTF was to "deliver to Berlin, in a safe and efficient manner, the maximum tonnage possible, consistent with the combined resources of equipment and personnel made available."[39] In addition to combining the American and British airlift efforts, this order changed the overall concept of the airlift. "From now on, we were to get all the tonnage we could into the blockaded city. The sky was the limit. This would change the emphasis from utilization of planes to tonnage, from a daily quota to unlimited quotas. Thus, when there was unforeseen congestion in the corridors or on the Berlin airfields and some part of the operation had to slow down, an American C-54, with its ten tons of cargo, took precedence over an RAF Dakota, with three tons," Tunner stated.[40] Maximum tonnage was the goal for the remainder of the airlift.

Setting up CALTF was one of LeMay's final acts as commander of USAFE. In Tunner's final efficiency report, LeMay described him as a "dignified, mature, earnest and forceful officer who is exceptionally conscientious and industrious. He is frank, loyal, tenacious and dependable. He has a knack for organizing rapidly and pressing ceaselessly for greater efficiency and results. He has an unusual capacity for personal sustained effort. In my opinion, Tunner is today's outstanding expert in air transport techniques."[41] Unfortunately for Tunner, General LeMay's replacement did not feel the same.

"'What the hell is this, Tunner?' he demanded, waving the directive creating the Combined Airlift Task Force. 'What are you trying to do to me?'"[42] According to Tunner, when Lt Gen John Cannon took over as commander of USAFE, Cannon intended to run the Berlin airlift himself and was not pleased with the agreement made with the British.[43]

Unlike Tunner's relationship with LeMay, where Tunner received strong support and great freedom to coordinate and deal with airlift problems, Cannon wanted all administrative issues directed through his command. "My letter of instructions from General Cannon changed the situation immediately. From that day on I was specifically forbidden to coordinate with MATS, AMC [Air Materiel Command], and just about everybody else. From then on all contact with other commands had to be made through USAFE headquarters."[44] The problem with this new arrangement was that airlift requests for facility and airfield improvements, necessary equipment and supplies, and additional or specialized personnel were typically bogged down in USAFE red tape.

Cannon and Tunner also clashed over the balance between Berlin airlift personnel requirements and troop morale. The majority of personnel assigned to the airlift were on temporary duty, and their tours had been extended more than once. Many wanted to go home. According to Tunner, General Cannon liked to be known as a good fellow. "He always wore a big smile, and he liked to go around listening to the troubles of the GI's. If the story was good enough, he'd send the man home regardless of his duties, or how long he had been in Europe. Word of this got around, and the more members of the Task Force began to think of Uncle Joe Cannon as sympathetic and kind-hearted and fair, the more their commander, I, became by contrast harsh and cold and a miserable guy to work for."[45] Cannon's leadership actions not only strained the relationship between Tunner and his men, but Cannon often sent men home that Tunner considered critical. Things soon changed.

On Christmas Eve, Secretary of the Air Force, Stuart Symington and Gen Jimmy Doolittle came to visit, and General Tunner briefed them on the airlift's many difficulties. "On Christmas Day I took him over the Rhine-Main air base to show him the operation. General Cannon met us there. Symington covered practically every square foot of the working section of the base, introducing himself to the men, putting them at their ease, and then asking pertinent and intelligent questions. Thus he learned at first hand, from the men themselves, many of the unpleasant living conditions that I had been screaming my head off to USAFE headquarters about but which had never gotten to the Secretary."[46]

When the tour was over, Symington told Tunner that he wanted a detailed report on the airlift's problems. Tunner and his staff spent several days working on a document entitled "Supply and Maintenance Problems—First Airlift Task Force," that addressed many of the airlift's difficulties. Symington and Cannon both received copies.[47] According to Tunner:

> From then on our problems in the areas of housing, inspections, and shortages of supplies were of far lesser significance. A rotation system was set up by Air Force headquarters to relieve the onerous extended-TDY situation. . . . It was still somewhat difficult operating under an unsympathetic command, and I am still convinced that we could have performed our mission more successfully had we had greater authority to run our own show, but at least from then on we had sufficient tools to work with.[48]

While Symington's visit vastly improved the airlift, it did not help the relationship between Cannon and Tunner. Tunner reported, "I never had a pleasant encounter with him all the time I was there."[49] Cannon made clear his opinion of Tunner in his efficiency report. Cannon described Tunner as "a rather conflicting personality whose first, last, and every thought is built around air transport. The most important and fruitful years of his service life have been spent therein, to the exclusion of other required essentials for the Air Force officer balanced career. He is industrious, positive, aggressive and determined, but stubborn, blunt and tactless, and, at times, unpredictable and vindictive. He does not inspire loyalty in his staff towards a higher headquarters."[50] Tunner considered their conflicting personalities as simply the "differences between combat people and transport people."[51]

Despite his difficulties with General Cannon, Tunner continued to drive the airlift forward. To offset personnel shortages during the early months of 1949, Tunner used Germans in maintenance, cargo handling, and administrative operations. There were eventually 80 German mechanics assigned to each squadron (see figure 9).[52] According to Tunner, "They were all first-class mechanics . . . and were a great deal of help in maintaining the airplanes." Tunner went on to say: "This is what you can learn from experience. You can do these things. Everybody I talked to at USAFE Headquarters said, 'Oh, you are going to regret this, taking the Germans on. You are going to regret it, because they will throw things into your machinery, and they'll sabotage you.' I said, 'Nonsense. They are just as interested as I am in getting those people in Berlin fed.' We never had a bit of sabotage of any kind whatsoever."[53]

German workers stood out in most areas where they participated. *The Task Force Times* ran a story highlighting a German

Figure 9. C-54 engine maintenance. (Reproduced from Combined Airlift Task Force, History, "Photos of the Berlin Air Lift, 572.08, July–August 1948, 00241465, AFHRA.")

unloading crew that emptied a C-54 aircraft of 20,000 pounds of coal in six minutes and 26 seconds.[54] Another story describes a German radio technician who designed an alarm device for signaling airway navigation beacon failures.[55] An official CALTF report concluded that "the utilization of indigenous personnel in support of an air transport operation has been highly successful," and their use "should not be overlooked in any future undertaking."[56]

With improved weather conditions in March and April, Berliners looked to the sky to see a steady stream of aircraft flowing into the city. According to Tunner,

> Its mere inception, even in its first unorganized beginning, helped the people's morale in that it was a daring innovation and something to talk about. It helped dispel the cold fear in the hearts of those who would never forget the Soviet looting and raping that the Western powers

would depart and leave them to the Soviets. It helped dispel the fear of hunger, and it even helped dispel the fear of another war. For the Berliners could see that this was a clever, nonviolent way of circumventing the blockade.[57]

However, the question still remained—could the airlift eventually break the Soviet blockade?

Though the lines on CALTF's total tonnage airlifted and aircraft utilization charts were rising, and those on the aircraft turnaround time and unloading time charts were falling, Tunner did not rest on his laurels.[58] Harnessing the spirit of competition demonstrated on the Hump and earlier in the airlift, Tunner directed a 24-hour tonnage surge to Berlin on 16 April 1949, Easter Sunday. During what became known as the Easter Parade, CALTF flew 1,398 flights with no accidents and delivered 12,940 tons to Berlin.[59]

General Tunner stated, "It was that day, that Easter Sunday, I'm sure, that broke the back of the Berlin blockade. From then on we never fell below nine thousand tons a day; the land blockade was pointless."[60] The Soviets seemed to agree, and on 5 May issued the following statement: "All restrictions imposed since March 1, 1948, by the Government of the Union of Soviet Socialist Republics on communications, transportation, and trade between Berlin and the western zones of Germany and between the Eastern zone and the western zones will be removed on May 12, 1949."[61] The airlift continued through September 1949, establishing stockpiles of reserves within the city. When the airlift ended, an impressive 276,926 flights had delivered 2,323,067 tons to the city of Berlin.[62]

Notes

1. Donovan, *Bridge in the Sky*, 4.
2. Ibid., 8. French participation in the occupation of Germany and the administration of Berlin would occur at a later time.
3. Miller, *To Save a City*, 4.
4. Donovan, *Bridge in the Sky*, 15.
5. Miller, *To Save a City*, 12.
6. Jackson, *The Berlin Airlift*, 34–36.
7. Miller, *To Save a City*, 6.
8. Collier, *Bridge Across the Sky*, 48–50.
9. Miller, *To Save a City*, 7–8.
10. Ibid., 33.

Air University

Stephen R. Lorenz, Lt Gen, Commander

**Air Force Doctrine Development
and Education Center**

Allen G. Peck, Maj Gen, Commander

Air Force Research Institute

John A. Shaud, PhD, Gen, USAF, Retired, Director

4

"When You Get a Job to Do, Do It"

The Airpower Leadership of Lt Gen William H. Tunner

David S. Hanson
Lieutenant Colonel, USAF

11. Jackson, *The Berlin Airlift*, 43.
12. Donovan, *Bridge in the Sky*, 40.
13. Jackson, *The Berlin Airlift*, 67.
14. Combined Airlift Task Force, *A Report on the Airlift Berlin Mission*, 12.
15. Jackson, *The Berlin Airlift*, 67; and Pearcy, *Berlin Airlift*, 33.
16. Tunner, *Over the Hump*, 160.
17. Tunner, oral history interview, 95–96.
18. Tunner, *Over the Hump*, 165.
19. Ibid., 163–64.
20. Donovan, *Bridge in the Sky*, 110.
21. Ibid., 110–11.
22. Combined Airlift Task Force, *A Report on Airlift Berlin Mission*, 12–13.
23. Miller, *To Save a City*, 115.
24. Ibid., 116.
25. Tunner, *Over the Hump*, 173.
26. *Aviation Operations*, A Special Study, 21–22.
27. Tunner, oral history interview, 97–98.
28. Donovan, *Bridge in the Sky*, 119.
29. Miller, *To Save a City*, 91, 119.
30. Collier, *Bridge Across the Sky*, 111–12.
31. Ibid., 122.
32. Tunner, Over the Hump, 178.
33. Tunner, oral history interview, 98–99.
34. Combined Airlift Task Force, History, vol. 1, March 1949, 4.
35. Donovan, *Bridge in the Sky*, 126.
36. Tunner, *Over the Hump*, 209.
37. Ibid., 186.
38. Donovan, *Bridge in the Sky*, 124.
39. Combined Airlift Task Force, Air Headquarters, British Air Forces of Occupation (Germany), Royal Air Force (RAF); Headquarters, United States Air Forces in Europe; Air Marshal Sir Arthur P. M. Saunders and Lt Gen Curtis E. LeMay. 18–19.
40. Tunner, *Over the Hump*, 187.
41. WD AGO Form No. 67, 28 July 1948–18 October 1948.
42. Tunner, *Over the Hump*, 189.
43. Tunner, oral history interview, 101.
44. Tunner, *Over the Hump*, 190.
45. Ibid., 191.
46. Ibid., 196.
47. Donovan, *Bridge in the Sky*, 160.
48. Tunner, *Over the Hump*, 197.
49. Tunner, oral history interview, 102.
50. AF Form No. 78, 21 March 1949.
51. Tunner, *Over the Hump*, 189.
52. Combined Airlift Task Force, *A Report on Airlift Berlin Mission*, 23.
53. Tunner, oral history interview, 92–93.
54. "Rhein Main Crew," *Task Force Times*.

55. "German Radio Operator," *Task Force Times*.
56. Combined Airlift Task Force, *A Report on Airlift Berlin Mission*, 96.
57. Tunner, *Over the Hump*, 217.
58. Combined Airlift Task Force, *A Report on Airlift Berlin Mission*, 87–93.
59. Combined Airlift Task Force, History, vol. 1, 5.
60. Tunner, *Over the Hump*, 222.
61. Donovan, *Bridge in the Sky*, 196.
62. Tunner, *Over the Hump*, 222.

Chapter 6

Summary and Critique

*Good Leaders are people who have a passion to suc-
ceed. . . . To become successful leaders, we must first
learn that no matter how good the technology or how
shiny the equipment, people-to-people relations get
things done in our organizations. People are the assets
that determine our success or failure.*

—Gen Ronald R. Fogleman

The story of Lt Gen William H. Tunner's leadership development provides a means for understanding his life, character,
and the challenges he faced. Studied through the components
of Air Force leadership doctrine, Tunner's past paints a portrait
of a tightly focused and highly driven air transportation expert
who made great contributions to the airlift element of airpower.
However, Tunner was far from perfect, with his "first, last, and
every thought . . . built around air transport," and lacking the
essentials required for a balanced career.[1] Was Tunner a successful Air Force leader? The leadership components described
in AFDD 1-1 and the proposed Air Force Leadership Framework illustrated in figure 10 provide a structure for answering
this question.

Experience

Tunner's early years as a junior officer provided a wealth of
education, training, and operational experience, and gave him a
sense of how air transportation differed from other forms of airpower. Tunner's military education and training began with four
years at West Point followed by a year of flight school training to
become an Air Corps pilot. Later, he sharpened his understanding of Army tactics while supporting the US Army Infantry School
and Air Corps airpower thinking as a student at ACTS.

While excelling at some jobs and failing at others, Tunner's
early military career provided him with the depth of experience

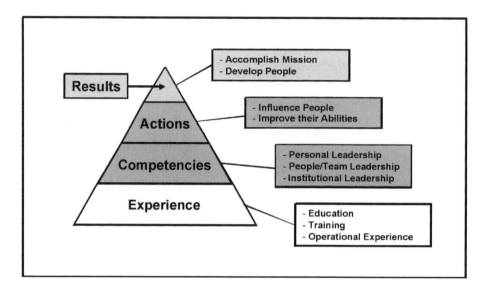

Figure 10. Air Force Leadership Framework (Proposed). (Adapted from AFDD 1-1, Leadership and Force Development, 18 February 2006.)

required for effective leadership. His first transport flight, recruiting reserve pilots, and weekend aircraft ferrying all provided Tunner with first-hand knowledge of the problems air transportation faced. The difficulties of scheduling aircrews and maintaining aircraft, the challenges of building airfields and resupplying forces, and the complications associated with running an air base exposed him to important aspects of the air transportation mission. As Tunner's responsibility increased, his education, training, and operational experience aided in developing his leadership competencies and influencing his leadership actions. To this point in his career, Tunner had yet to serve in an air transport assignment, though his early years undoubtedly provided him with a strong foundation for leadership in military air transport.

Competencies

Assigned as the personnel officer to the newly established Ferrying Command, Tunner developed and exercised his personal leadership competencies. Key to developing basic competencies were his skills in communicating effectively with Col Robert Olds and various members of the Air Staff, and his ability to adapt to challenging conditions and make sound decisions. Tunner's ambition shows in his recommendation to reorganize the command and fill a key leadership position with himself.

Next, when Tunner commanded the domestic division of Ferrying Command he transitioned to developing and using the people/team competencies of leading people and fostering relationships. He provided early guidance to his staff, stressing the importance of teamwork and effective communication. While encouraging his staff to do their jobs, Tunner insisted that they bring all important information and difficult problems directly to him. This desire for control was consistent in Tunner's commands. He demonstrated a strong capacity for effectively working with outside agencies to improve the process of qualifying, training, and educating domestic division aircrews.

Finally, as Tunner commanded ferrying and training operations for Air Transport Command he focused on implementing institutional level competencies. Commanding Ferrying Division, Tunner understood his organization's contribution to the war effort and fostered a variety of innovations. The creation of flying safety programs, hiring of women pilots, and establishment of a rapid air-transport service all originated within Tunner's Ferrying Division. Though examined over a relatively short period of time, the maturation of Tunner's leadership competencies is readily apparent throughout his involvement in the ferrying business. These competencies would influence Tunner's actions during future commands.

Actions

In August 1944, General Tunner took command of a struggling Hump airlift operation and began the dual mission of increasing tonnage and decreasing accidents. Upon arriving in theater, Tunner and his staff effectively surveyed the situation, identified problems, and instituted initiatives designed to improve airlift efficiency and safety. Though Tunner is typically credited with the Hump airlift mission success, it was his select staff that took his leadership actions and made them reality within the ICD.

59

To accomplish the mission, Tunner focused his actions on influencing Hump airlift personnel through personal discipline, military standards, and effective communication. With an understanding of their influence on mission performance, Tunner required clean facilities, regular inspections, and formal parades to inject military discipline and standards. He changed the aircrew rotation policy to reduce pilot fatigue and increase expertise. Tunner also pushed a robust flight safety program and declared to ICD personnel that tonnage would not take priority over safety.

Tunner concentrated his actions on instituting specialized training programs and initiatives in both aircraft maintenance and flying operations. His emphasis on phased-flight training helped new pilots gradually acclimate themselves to the Hump operating environment. His focus on jungle indoctrination aided in building aircrew confidence and capability in surviving after a bailout or forced landing. These two training efforts likely saved many lives and aircraft. Tunner and his staff recognized that the number of aircraft available and the amount of cargo each aircraft could carry limited tonnage capability. To overcome these limits, he focused on improvements in maintenance and flight operations geared towards helping ICD personnel work more efficiently. While Tunner's concept of production line maintenance increased efficiency, it was his close supervision that drove the process forward.

Tunner believed that "each plane must be flying, be undergoing maintenance, or be in the process of loading or unloading every second of every day."[2] He remained committed to efficiency as a means for success in every operation he led and proved quick to knock down obstacles. When conflicts arose over airlift aircraft in China, Tunner quickly took the problem over General Chennault's head, directly to the theater commander. According to General Tunner, "I didn't make friends that way, but I got my job done."[3]

Tunner's single-minded focus on getting the job done permeated his actions and had repercussions up and down his chain of command. While he relied on his select staff to complement his strengths and offset his weaknesses, he was autocratic, and thus failed to let others gain leadership experience. This method worked when he was in the driver's seat. When he was not available though, as with the Orient Project, the operation quickly fell apart. This is both a testament to Tunner as a mission leader and a reflection of his failure in developing future air transportation leaders capable of taking his place.

Though nearly three years would pass between the end of the Hump airlift and the start of the Berlin Airlift, the expertise for running a large-scale air-transport operation remained primarily with Tunner. Recognizing early USAFE mistakes in running the Berlin Airlift, Tunner pushed for MATS involvement, became the commander, and left his position as deputy commander of MATS while his boss was away on a trip. Having little interest in the opinions of others, he focused on the mission to provide Berlin with the maximum tonnage possible. As Tunner took command, his intent was to provide the Berlin Airlift with similar practices, techniques, and standards that achieved success on the Hump. Unlike the Hump, his actions were weighted heavily towards influencing rather than improving personnel.

Tunner's early Airlift efforts focused on efficient ground and air operations. First, he established ground operating procedures that allowed crews to stay with their aircraft, met their return flight requirements, and reduced ground turn-around time. Next, in response to Black Friday, Tunner and his staff standardized flight rules, mission profiles, and landing minimums in order to improve airlift efficiency and safety. Finally, while commanding both the American and British airlift efforts, he orchestrated the optimum use of western air bases, air routes, and aircraft for increased airlift efficiency. Together, these actions helped produce Tunner's "conveyor belt" type operation.

Tunner stressed different motivations as means of influencing his troops. Once his standing operating procedures were in place, he devoted time to meeting with his flyers and incorporating their suggestions into airlift operations. This provided Tunner with first-hand information and demonstrated that he valued constructive inputs. He also motivated others through intimidation. During a meeting with his staff, Tunner said, "Now look, we came here to work. I'm not asking you men to put in twenty-four-hours a day, but dammit, if I can do eighteen hours a day, you can do fifteen."[4] He checked up on airlift components and operations unannounced. For Tunner, both positive and negative motivation served as means for influencing airlift efficiency and results.

61

As with the Hump, Tunner's sharp focus on the airlift's mission brought him into conflict with other Air Force leaders. He handled conflicts with General Cannon by bypassing his chain of command and taking issues directly to Secretary Symington. His loyalty rested with the mission and those who accomplished it.

Results

Tunner produced results during the Hump and Berlin airlifts that command respect and prove his success as a leader. With regard to mission execution, he performed brilliantly in both operations. He leveraged his expert staff to execute his leadership actions and achieve his operational vision. From his firm supervision of maintenance in Memphis to making the late-night rounds at Tempelhof, Tunner maintained a close, personal relationship with the operations he led. His innate understanding of airpower and his unique talent as an air mobility expert allowed him to achieve tremendous results with limited resources.

At times, Tunner's sharp mission focus blinded him to his leadership responsibility to develop future leaders. Though loyal to his staff, Tunner's mission focus prevented him from developing air-transportation leaders. He highlighted the important role his "old reliables" played in the airlift operations he commanded, but limited his praise for them to their ability to follow his instructions. Tunner never recognized another airlift leader within his commands, nor identified anyone capable of taking his place. This failure to develop air-transport leaders contributed to the collapse of the Orient Project and limited the Air Force's options for future airlift operations. As a result, and perhaps by design, Tunner was consistently chosen to command major air-transport operations. This lack of emphasis on developing leaders was a weakness in Tunner's leadership.

In sum, future generations of Airmen can learn a great deal from General Tunner's leadership during the Hump and Berlin airlifts. His focus and drive contributed to the rapid development of military air transportation and the unprecedented success of both airlift operations. His failures, however, illustrate how a triumphant mission leader can still falter as an Air Force leader. In the end though, Tunner must be counted as a successful Air Force leader given the scale of his contributions.

Notes

1. AF Form No. 78, 21 March 1949.
2. Tunner, *Over the Hump*, 118.
3. Tunner, oral history interview, 54–58.
4. Tunner, *Over the Hump*, 167.

Bibliography

Air Corps Ferrying Command. "Operating Instruction: Policy," 10 July 1941. 168.7158-253, 7 October 1941–4 July 1949, 01096920. Air Force Historical Research Agency, Maxwell AFB, AL (AFHRA). Microfilm roll number 43016, frames 6–59.

Air Corps Primary Flying School, Brooks Field, San Antonio, Texas. "Final Grade Sheet, 2d Lt William H. Tunner, 28 June 1928." 141.290-76 Folder 2, 9 June 1928–31 May 1960, 01151753, 67. AFHRA. https://132.60.137.32/g$/PEP/Tunner%20William%20H%2076-2.pdf.

Air Force Doctrine Document (AFDD) 1. *Air Force Basic Doctrine*, 17 November 2003.

AFDD 1-1. *Leadership and Force Development*, 18 February 2006.

Air Force Form (AF Form) No. 78, 21 March 1949, *Air Force General Officer Efficiency Report*. "Maj Gen William H. Tunner, 27 May 1949." 141.290-76 Folder 1, 9 June 1928–31 May 1960, 01151752, 323–25. AFHRA. https://132.60.137.32/g$/PEP/Tunner%20William%20H%2076-1.pdf.

AF Form No. 78, 21 March 1949. *Air Force General Officer Efficiency Report*. "Maj Gen William H. Tunner, 5 November 1949." 141.290-76 Folder 4, 9 June 1928–31 May 1960, 01151752, 319–21. AFHRA. https://132.60.137.32/g$/PEP/Tunner%20William%20H%2076-1.pdf.

Air Transport Command. Memorandum. "Recommendation for award of the Distinguished Service Medal to Brigadier General William H. Tunner, 22 July 1944." 141.290-76 Folder 1, 9 June 1928–31 May 1960, 01151752, 105–9. AFHRA. https://132.60.137.32/g$/PEP/Tunner%20William%20H%2076-1.pdf.

———. Memorandum. "Recommendation for Bronze Oak Leaf Cluster to the Distinguished Service Medal," 15 January 1946. 141.290-76 Folder 1, 9 June 1928–31 May 1960, 01151752, 31–43. AFHRA. https://132.60.137.32/g$/PEP/Tunner%20William%20H%2076-1.pdf.

———. Memorandum. "To Commanding General, Army Air Forces (Thru Channels); Subject: Promotion of Officer, 3 April 1943." 141.290-76 Folder 2, 9 June 1928–31 May

1960, 01151753, 165. AFHRA. https://132.60.137.32/g$/PEP/Tunner%20William%20H%2076-2.pdf.

————. *The Origins of the Ferrying Division*, 3 vols. May through December 1941. 301.01 V.1, 2–3, 29 May 1941–30 September 1945, 00180381. AFHRA. Microfilm roll A3011/5526, frames 103–1384.

Appendix. "Office of the Chief of the Air Corps, For the Assistant Secretary of War for Air, Subject: Airplane Ferry Service for the British," 298–99. Microfilm roll A3011/5526, frames 421–22. In Air Transport Command. *The Origins of the Ferrying Division*, vol. 1, *The Air Corps Ferrying Command, May through December 1941*. 301.01 V.1, 29 May 1941–30 September 1945, 00180381. AFHRA.

————. "Organization of the Air Corp Ferrying Command (Domestic Wing), 28 December 1941," 802. Microfilm roll A3011/5526, frame 964. In Air Transport Command. *The Origins of the Ferrying Division*, vol. 2, *The Domestic Wing, January through June 1942*. 301.01 V.2, 29 May 1941–30 September 1945, 00180382. AFHRA.

————. Col Robert Olds, Commander, Air Corps Ferrying Command. Memorandum. "To Chief of the Air Corps; Subject: General Plan for Movement of British Aircraft from Factories to England, 23 June 1941," 326–33. Microfilm roll A3011/5526, frames 450–57. In Air Transport Command. *The Origins of the Ferrying Division*, vol. 1, *The Air Corps Ferrying Command, May through December 1941*. 301.01 V.1, 29 May 1941–30 September 1945, 00180381. AFHRA.

————. Col William H. Tunner, Commander, Ferrying Division, Air Transport Command. Memorandum. "To Commanding General of the Army Air Forces; Subject: Difficulties with A-31 Aircraft, 23 December 1942," 235–37. Microfilm roll A3011/5526, frames 1329–31. In Air Transport Command. *The Origins of the Ferrying Division*, vol. 3, *The Domestic Wing, January through June 1942*. 301.01 V.3, 29 May 1941–30 September 1945, 00180383. AFHRA.

————. General Orders No. 3, Headquarters, ACFC [Air Corps Ferrying Command], 30 December 1941," 805. Microfilm roll A3011/5526, frame 967. In Air Transport Command. *The Origins of the Ferrying Division*, vol. 2, *The Domestic Wing,*

January through June 1942. 301.01 V.2, 29 May 1941–30 September 1945, 00180382. AFHRA.

———. General Orders No. 8, Headquarters, Army Air Forces, 20 June 1942, 915. Microfilm roll A3011/5526, frame 1078. In Air Transport Command. *The Origins of the Ferrying Division,* vol. 2, *The Domestic Wing, January through June 1942.* 301.01 V.2, 29 May 1941–30 September 1945, 00180382.

———. Lt Col William H. Tunner, Commander, Domestic Division, Air Corps Ferrying Command. Memorandum. "To: General Olds; Subject: Requirements for Position of Civilian Pilot (male) with the Air Corps Ferrying Command, 30 January 1942," 832. Microfilm roll A3011/5526, frame 994. In Air Transport Command. *The Origins of the Ferrying Division,* vol. 2, *The Domestic Wing, January through June 1942.* 301.01 V.2, 29 May 1941–30 September 1945, 00180382. AFHRA.

———. War Department Circular 55-20, *Operations: Air Corps Ferrying Command,* 30 June 1941, 334–5. Microfilm roll A3011/5526, frames 458–59. In Air Transport Command. *The Origins of the Ferrying Division,* vol. 1, *The Air Corps Ferrying Command, May through December 1941.* 301.01 V.1, 29 May 1941–30 September 1945, 00180381. AFHRA.

Army Air Forces, India Burma Theater. Memorandum. "To: Commanding General, India–Burma Division, Air Transport Command; Subject: Commendation, 4 August 1945." 141.290-76 Folder 1, 9 June 1928–31 May 1960, 01151752, 3. AFHRA. https://132.60.137.32/g$/PEP/Tunner%20William%20H%2076-1.pdf.

Austin, Lt Col James W., deputy assistant chief of staff, personnel, India China Division, Air Transport Command. Memorandum. "To Commanding Officers, Army Air Forces Base Units; Subject: Revision of Air Crew Rotation Policy, 23 March 1945." In United States Air Forces in Europe. "Karache [*sic*] Investigation, End of War." 168.7158-278, 1945, 01096945. AFHRA. Microfilm roll 43017, frame 303–6.

Aviation Operations: A Special Study of Operation Vittles. 168.92, April 1949, 00127347. AFHRA. Microfilm roll A1937/3401, frames 4–123.

Brown, Shannon A. "The Sources of Leadership Doctrine in the Air Force." *Air and Space Power Journal* 16, no. 4 (Winter 2002): 38.

"Chapter 1, The Establishment of the Ferrying Command, May and June 1941: The First Directives on Ferrying," 15-7. Microfilm roll A3011/5526, frames 137–39. In Air Transport Command. *The Origins of the Ferrying Division*, vol. 1, *The Air Corps Ferrying Command, May through December 1941*. 301.01 V.1, 29 May 1941–30 September 1945, 00180381. AFHRA.

"Chapter 5, Operations of the Ferrying Command, June to December 1941: Operational Plan and Methods of Ferrying," 243–59. Microfilm roll A3011/5526, frames 365–81. In Air Transport Command. *The Origins of the Ferrying Division*, vol. 1, *The Air Corps Ferrying Command, May Through December 1941*. 301.01 V.1, 29 May 1941–30 September 1945, 00180381. AFHRA.

"Chapter 8, Headquarters and other Organizational Developments, Spring 1942, the Domestic Wing, the Groups: Personnel Problems 1, Personnel Problems, Stationing Pilots," 573–77. Microfilm roll A3011/5526, frames 732–36. In Air Transport Command. *The Origins of the Ferrying Division*, vol. 2, *The Domestic Wing, January through June 1942*. 301.01 V.2, 29 May 1941–30 September 1945, 00180382. AFHRA.

———: Personnel Problems 2, Use of Civilian Pilots," 578–604. Microfilm roll A3011/5526, frames 767–75. In Air Transport Command. *The Origins of the Ferrying Division*, vol. 2, *The Domestic Wing, January through June 1942*. 301.01 V.2, 29 May 1941–30 September 1945, 00180382. AFHRA.

———: Personnel Problems 4, Training," 608–16. Microfilm roll A3011/5526, frames 767–75. In Air Transport Command. *The Origins of the Ferrying Division*, vol. 2, *The Domestic Wing, January through June 1942*. 301.01 V.2, 29 May 1941–30 September 1945, 00180382. AFHRA.

Coira, Louis E. Oral history interview by Dr. James C. Hasdorff, San Antonio, TX, 17 July 1989. K239.512-1865, 25 April 1916 -17 July 1989, 01128757.AFHRA.https://132.60.137.32/g$/OHI/COIRA%20LOUIS%20E%201865v0.pdf.

Collier, Richard. Bridge across the Sky. New York: McGraw-Hill, 1978.

Combined Airlift Task Force. *A Report on the Airlift Berlin Mission.* 572.101B, 26 June 1948–1 August 1949, 30 August 1949, 01006566. AFHRA. Microfilm roll 30785, frame 575–674.

———. Air Headquarters, British Air Forces of Occupation (Germany), Royal Air Force (RAF); Headquarters, United States Air Forces in Europe; Air Marshal Sir Arthur P. M. Saunders and Lt Gen Curtis E. LeMay. Letter. "Subject: Letter Directive for a Combined USAF–RAF Airlift Task Force; To: Major General William H. Tunner," undated. In History, vol 1, 18–9. 572.02 V.2, March 1949, 00241455. AFHRA. Microfilm roll C5111/8244, frames 595–96.

———. History, 2 vols. 572.02 V.1 and 2, March 1949, 00241455 and 00241456. AFHRA. Microfilm roll C5111/8244, frames 543–1031.

———. "Photos of the Berlin Air Lift." 572.08, July–August 1948, 00241465. AFHRA. Microfilm roll C5113/8246, frames 35–63.

Craven, Wesley Frank and James Lea Cate, eds. *The Army Air Forces in World War II*, vol. 5, *The Pacific: Matterhorn to Nagasaki, June 1944 to August 1945*. Washington, DC: Office of Air Force History, 1953.

———. *The Army Air Forces in World War II*, vol. 7, *Services around the World*. Washington, DC: Office of Air Force History, 1953.

Dobson, Alan P. *US Wartime Aid to Britain 1940–1946.* New York: St. Martin's Press, 1986.

Donovan, Frank. *Bridge in the Sky.* New York: David McKay Company, Inc., 1968.

Flight "B," 16th Observation Squadron, Air Corps. Memorandum. "To: 1st Lt William H. Tunner; Subject: Commendation, 13 May 1938." 141.290-76 Folder 4, 9 June 1928–31 May 1960, 01151752, 366. AFHRA. https://132.60.137.32/g$/PEP/Tunner%20William%20H%2076-4.pdf.

Form No. 0337.A, Adjutant General's Office, 10 January 1925. "Historical Record of Officer: Statement of Officer upon Appointment in Regular Army," 9 June 1928. 141.290-76 Folder 2, 9 June 1928–31 May 1960, 01151753, 61–3. AFHRA.

https://132.60.137.32/g$/PEP/Tunner%20William%20H%2076-2.pdf.

Gorgas Hospital, Health Department, Canal Zone, The Panama Canal. Memorandum, "Abstract of Clinical Records, Lt William H. Tunner, Ancon, Canal Zone, 15 September 1936." 141.290-76 Folder 4, 9 June 1928–31 May 1960, 01151755, 55–7. AFHRA. https://132.60.137.32/g$/PEP/Tunner%20William%20H%2076-4.pdf.

India-China Division, Air Transport Command. "Arriving Pilots Given Training in Hump School: Four Phases Include Pre-Flight, Transition." *Hump Express*, 3 May 1945. http://cbi-theater-9.home.comcast.net/hump_express/hump050345.html.

———. "Division Is Big Employer of Civilians; Many Are Specialists." *Hump Express*, 15 February 1945. http://cbi-theater-9.home.comcast.net/hump_express/hump021545.html.

———. "Hump's Worst Weather Bats Planes About: Winds up to 125 M.P.H. Harass Fliers as Equipment Goes Out, Ships Tip." *Hump Express*, 25 January 1945. http://cbi-theater-9.home.comcast.net/hump_express/hump012545.html.

———. "Kemi-Nodi Sojourners Learn About Jungle Life While They Have Fun." *Hump Express*, 8 February 1945. http://cbi-theater-9.home.comcast.net/hump_express/hump020845.html.

———. "New Policy for Rotation of Air Crews Calls for At Least One Year of Service with Division: Routine Changed to Decrease Tension and Strain of Piling up many Hours in Short Time; 750 Hours of Hump Time Required." *Hump Express*, 29 March 1945. http://cbi-theater-9.home.comcast.net/hump_express/hump032945.html.

Jackson, Robert. *The Berlin Airlift*. Wellingborough, UK: Thorsons Publishing Group, 1988.

La Farge, Lt Col Oliver. *The Eagle in the Egg*. Boston: Houghton Mifflin, 1949.

LeMay, Curtis E. *Mission with LeMay*. Garden City, NJ: Doubleday & Company, Inc., 1965.

———. Oral history interview by Col Bill Peck, USAF, San Antonio, TX, March 1965. K239.0512-785, 1930–March 1965, 01000342. AFHRA. https://132.60.137.32/g$/OHI/LEMAY%20C%20E%200785v0.pdf.

"Major General William Henry Tunner, USAF, 374A (Record of Service as of 3 July 1953)." 141.290-76 Folder 3, 9 June 1928–31 May 1960, 01151754, 147. AFHRA. https://132.60.137.32/g$/PEP/Tunner%20William%20H%2076-3.pdf.

Meilinger, Col Philip S., USAF. "American Air Power Biography, William H. Tunner." *Air and Space Power Journal.* http://www.airpower.maxwell.af.mil/airchronicles/cc/tunn.html.

Memorandum. "To: Commanding General, Army Air Forces. Subject: Recommendation for Award of Legion of Merit; 21 September 1943." 141.290-76 Folder 1, 9 June 1928–31 May 1960, 01151752, 73. AFHRA. https://132.60.137.32/g$/PEP/Tunner%20William%20H%2076-1.pdf.

Miller, Roger G. *To Save a City.* College Station: Texas A&M University Press, 2000.

Office of Deputy Command, 20th Air Force, Brig Gen Joseph Smith. Letter. "Brigadier General William H. Tunner, Commanding General, India–China Div. [Division] ATC," 4 July 1945. 141.290-76 Folder 1, 9 June 1928–31 May 1960, 01151752, 151. AFHRA. https://132.60.137.32/g$/PEP/Tunner%20William%20H%2076-1.pdf.

Office of the Chief of the Air Corps. "Personnel Orders, No. 40: Extract, 3. Capt William H. Tunner, 17 February 1941." 141.290-76 Folder 2, 9 June 1928–31 May 1960, 01151753, 165. AFHRA. https://132.60.137.32/g$/PEP/Tunner%20William%20H%2076-2.pdf.

———. Memorandum. "To: Major William H. Tunner; Subject: Orders, 31 May 1941." 141.290-76 Folder 2, 9 June 1928–31May1960,01151753,169.AFHRA.https://132.60.137.32/g$/PEP/Tunner%20William%20H%2076-2.pdf.

Office of the Chief of Staff, Military Intelligence Division, Maj Gen Clayton Bissel. Letter. "Brig. Gen. William H. Tunner, Hqrs [Headquarters], ATC [Air Transport Command], India–Burma Theater," 6 July 1945. 141.290-76 Folder 1, 9 June 1928–31 May 1960, 01151752, 333. AFHRA. https://132.60.137.32/g$/PEP/Tunner%20William%20H%2076-1.pdf.

Office of the Intelligence and Security Officer, 1306th Army Air Forces Base Unit, India Wing, India-China Division, Air Transport Command. "Special Intelligence Report, 13 September 1945." In United States Air Forces in Europe. "Karache [*sic.*] Investigation, End of War." 168.7158-278, 1945, 01096945. AFHRA. Microfilm roll 3016, frames 311–23.

Pearcy, Arthur. *Berlin Airlift.* Shrewsbury, MA: Airlife, 1997.

Powell, Stewart. "The Berlin Airlift." *Air Force Magazine Online*, June 1998. www.afa.org/magazine/June1998/0698berlin .asp.

"Report of Decorations Board," 28 July 1944. 141.290-76 Folder 1, 9 June 1928–31 May 1960, 01151752, 111. AFHRA. https://132.60.137.32/g$/PEP/Tunner%20William%20H %2076-1.pdf.

Scott, Beth F., Lt Col James C. Rainey and Capt Andrew W. Hunt. *The Logistics of War: A Historical Perspective.* Maxwell AFB, AL: Air Force Logistics Management Agency, 2000.

2nd Ferrying Group History. GP-FER-2-SU-PE, 1937–8 May 1992, 01148320. AFHRA.

VI Bomber Command History. K466.04, 1941–31 August 1945, 1 April 1995, 01145207. AFHRA.

Task Force Times. "German Radio Operator Designs Alarm Device for Beacon Failure," 19 March 1949, 1. Microfilm roll C5111/8244, frame 999. In Combined Airlift Task Force. History, vol. 2. 572.02 V. 2, March 1949, 00241455. AFHRA.

———. "Hump and Lift," 26 March 1949, 1–2. Microfilm roll C5111/8244, frames 1003–4. In Combined Airlift Task Force. History, vol. 2. 572.02 V. 2, March 1949, 00241455. AFHRA.

———. "Rhein Main Crew Claims Record of 18 Minutes Turn-Around Time," 14 March 1949, 1. Microfilm roll C5111/8244, frame 997. In Combined Airlift Task Force. History, vol. 2. 572.02 V. 2, March 1949, 00241455. AFHRA.

Tunner, W. H. Oral history interview by Dr. James C. Hasdorff, Ware Neck, VA, 5–6 October 1976. K239.0512.911, 6 October 1976. 01033780. AFHRA. https://132.60.137.32/ g$/OHI/TUNNER%20A%20H%200912v0.pdf.

———. *Over the Hump.* Washington, DC: Office of Air Force History, 1964.

War Department (WD), Adjutant General's Office (AGO) Form No. 67, 1 May 1926, *Efficiency Report.* "2d Lt William H. Tunner, Rockwell Field, CA, 1 July 1930–30 June 1931."

141.290-76 Folder 1, 9 June 1928–31 May 1960, 01151752, 383–85. AFHRA. https://132.60.137.32/g$/PEP/Tunner %20William%20H%2076-1.pdf.

———, 1 May 1926. *Efficiency Report.* "2d Lt William H. Tunner, Rockwell Field, CA, 23 October 1931–27 February 1932." 141.290-76 Folder 1, 9 June 1928–31 May 1960, 01151752, 393–95. AFHRA. https://132.60.137.32/g$/PEP/Tunner %20William%20H%2076-1.pdf.

———, 1 February 1933. *Efficiency Report.* "2d Lt William H. Tunner, Rockwell Field, CA, 1 July 1933–30 June 1934." 141.290-76 Folder 1, 9 June 1928–31 May 1960, 01151752, 405–07. AFHRA. https://132.60.137.32/g$/PEP/Tunner %20William%20H%2076-1.pdf.

———, 1 February 1933. *Efficiency Report.* "1st Lt William H. Tunner, Rockwell Field, CA, 1 July 1935–25 September 1935." 141.290-76 Folder 1, 9 June 1928–31 May 1960, 01151752, 419–21. AFHRA. https://132.60.137.32/g$/ PEP/Tunner%20William%20H%2076-1.pdf.

———, 1 February 1933. *Efficiency Report.* "1st Lt William H. Tunner, Rockwell Field, CA, 26 September 1935–30 June 1936." 141.290-76 Folder 1, 9 June 1928–31 May 1960, 01151752, 423–5. AFHRA. https://132.60.137.32/g$/ PEP/Tunner%20William%20H%2076-1.pdf.

———, 1 January 1936. *Efficiency Report.* "1st Lt William H. Tunner, Rockwell Field, CA, 31 December 1936–21 April 1937." 141.290-76 Folder 1, 9 June 1928–31 May 1960, 01151752, 439–41. AFHRA. https://132.60.137.32/g$/PEP/Tunner %20William%20H%2076-1.pdf.

———, 1 July 1936. *Efficiency Report.* "Capt William H. Tunner, Rockwell Field, CA, 1 July 1938–30 June 1939." 141.290-76 Folder 4, 9 June 1928–31 May 1960, 01151752, 457–59. AFHRA. https://132.60.137.32/g$/PEP/Tunner %20William%20H%2076-1.pdf.

———, 1 July 1936. *Efficiency Report.* "Capt William H. Tunner, Rockwell Field, CA, 7 September 1939–5 December 1939." 141.290-76 Folder 2, 9 June 1928–31 May 1960, 01151752, 419–21. AFHRA. https://132.60.137.32/g$/ PEP/Tunner%20William%20H%2076-2.pdf.

———, 1 July 1947. *Efficiency Report.* "Maj Gen William H. Tunner, European Command, 28 July 1948–18 October 1948."

141.290-76 Folder 4, 9 June 1928–31 May 1960, 01151752, 279–81. AFHRA. https://132.60.137.32/g$/PEP/Tunner %20William%20H%2076-1.pdf.